JEZEBELLION

THE WARRIOR'S GUIDE TO
IDENTIFYING THE JEZEBEL SPIRIT

JEZEBELLION

THE WARRIOR'S GUIDE TO
IDENTIFYING THE JEZEBEL SPIRIT

TIFFANY BUCKNER

Anointed Fire House™

Jezebellion:
The Warrior's Guide to Identifying the Jezebel Spirit
by Tiffany Buckner

© 2017, Tiffany Buckner
www.tiffanybuckner.com
info@anointedfire.com

Published by Anointed Fire™ House
www.anointedfirehouse.com
Cover Design by Anointed Fire™ House
Author photograph by Dominique 'Chevon' Doyle
www.sochevon.com

ISBN-10: 0-9982507-7-5
ISBN-13: 978-0-9982507-7-9

I have tried to recreate events, locales and conversations from my memories of them. In order to maintain their anonymity in some instances, I have changed the names of individuals and places and I may have changed some identifying characteristics and details such as physical properties, occupations and places of residence.

Although the author and publisher have made every effort to ensure that the information in this book was correct at press time, the author and publisher do not assume and hereby disclaim any liability to any party for any loss, damage, or disruption caused by errors or omissions, whether such errors or omissions result from negligence, accident, or any other cause.

Table of Contents

Foreword

I have had my share of run-ins with the Jezebel spirit. Many years ago, I nearly lost everything to this heinous spirit (including my life). While sitting in my room one night, I found myself suffocating under the clutches of fear, intimidation and control. This foul spirit has destroyed families, dismantled ministries and disintegrated churches all because of the simple fact that God's people have been ignorant to her evil agenda. Years ago, I learned how to break free from the grip of this evil (albeit unseen) spirit.

In this masterful work, Jezebellion, Tiffany Buckner snatches the mask off of this evil spirit. Through a careful application of God's Word and personal stories, Tiffany helps the reader to identify, resist and break free from the power of the Jezebel spirit. With the crystal clarity of a seasoned veteran and the humility of a woman of God, she does what many have not been able to do: expose the wicked agenda of Jezebel while leading the believer on a path to lasting freedom. As you read, pay close attention. Examine yourself and allow the Holy Spirit to do a deep work within your own heart and mind. You will be challenged, strengthened, convicted, encouraged and transformed.

Dr. Kynan Bridges
Bestselling Author, Unmasking The Accuser
Senior Pastor, Grace & Peace Global Fellowship, Inc.

Preface

Case study. That's the term I heard when I was trying to figure out how to describe my encounters with the Jezebel spirit. Google defines the term "case study" this way: *a process or record of research in which detailed consideration is given to the development of a particular person, group, or situation over a period of time.* College students, psychologists and scientists are known to perform case studies. What they normally do is study the mindset, actions and reactions of a certain group of people or a class of living things. Nevertheless, my case study wasn't intentional—*not at least on my end.* I didn't purposely set out to study the Jezebel spirit; I was pretty much like a lab mouse being tossed onto a small, snake-infested island as an experiment. The fact that I survived it all is a testament of God's grace and mercy. Howbeit, one thing I realized in the midst of it all is that God did not toss me into this lesson; I pretty much volunteered for it, albeit, unknowingly. Of course, we are all vessels created by God. A vessel is a large ship or boat, so the best way to describe my life during this case study is... I was a wrecked soul. My sin caused me to shipwreck, but I didn't find myself on some physical island. My shipwreck was spiritual because I was a vessel of God who kept cruising between sin and righteousness. I shipwrecked in a mindset and it was in that mindset that I found myself in one of the most heated battles of my life. When I cried out to God and fully dedicated my life to Him, the battle grew more intense because I had to escape the fangs of the enemy one word at a time. What does this mean? Satan deceives God's people with one question at a time. He asks us, "Did God really tell you to do this?" or "Are you sure that you heard from God?" These questions are nothing but a formation of words designed to open us up to doubt. Because I didn't have enough Word in me to anchor me during the harsh storms of life, I found myself doing like a lot of believers do today: I found myself trying to take shortcuts to get around the storms of life and some of those shortcuts led me into some pretty dark places. Therefore, my recovery was nothing short of a rescue mission where I had to find myself and be led back into the will of God by the Word of God. I had to unburden myself of the self-imposed rules that I'd once weighed myself down with.

The 28th chapter of Acts tells a story that most of us are familiar with. That's the story of Apostle Paul being bitten by a viper (venomous snake). Paul had shipwrecked on a European island named Malta and that island was crawling with pagans.

Acts 28:1-6 (ESV): *After we were brought safely through, we then learned that the island was called Malta. The native people showed us unusual kindness, for they kindled a fire and welcomed us all, because it had begun to rain and was cold. When Paul had gathered a bundle of sticks and put them on the fire, a viper came out because of the heat and fastened on his hand. When the native people saw the creature hanging from his hand, they said to one another, "No doubt this man is a murderer. Though he has escaped from the sea, Justice has not allowed him to live." He, however, shook off the creature into the fire and suffered no harm. They were waiting for him to swell up or suddenly fall down dead. But when they had waited a long time and saw no misfortune come to him, they changed their minds and said that he was a god.*

In this story, we see that Paul was not only bitten by a venomous snake, but no one tried to help him survive the snake's bite. The reason for this is, the people of the land had beliefs similar to the belief in *karma*. They believed the summation of a man's life could be seen in both the way he lived and the way he died. Even though they didn't personally know Paul, they believed that the snake bite was synonymous with Paul having been a wicked man and therefore, his death would have been merited. When he did not die, they were astonished, so they came to another conclusion about Paul. They then believed that he was some sort of god. This is very similar to the way many believers reason today. What I've discovered is that the Island of Sin is full of pagans, some of whom identify themselves as Christians. Any time Jezebel is seen attacking a believer, most folks will stand on the sidelines and wait for that believer to either perish or become a Jezebel himself or herself. This is because Jezebel is an infectious spirit that spreads itself out through generational curses, pain, and ungodly soul ties. It is very similar to Hollywood's depiction of the infamous vampire. It lures its lovers into dark places with its beauty, charm and deceptive words. In the darkness, it unleashes its fangs and begins to drain the life out of its victims. Some of the victims emerge from the darkness as Jezebels, Ahabs, or other demonic spirits under the Baal principality. The rest of its victims never reemerge. I did come out of the darkness, but like most believers, the darkness was no longer outside of me; it was in me, and my deliverance from the darkness and everything that lurked therein was a lengthy process. Nevertheless, I was determined to become the vessel God designed me to be, so I fought against the darkness and I let the light of God begin to fill me up one word at a time. This was my pathway to deliverance.

In 2014 or 2015, the Lord told me that He was going to use me to write a book about the Jezebel spirit. He even gave me the title of the book, so it goes without saying, I wanted to fast-track the process and start writing right away. Nevertheless, I didn't have a peace about it. I'd written enough books by then to know that if I didn't feel that oh-so-familiar tugging on me to start writing right away, it was simply not my season to write on that particular subject. God was simply telling me to pay attention; that way, I could take the lessons I learned during my encounters with Jezebel and share them with the world. He was pretty much acknowledging that I was in the midst of a lesson—a case study of sorts—and I needed to focus on the path He used to bring me out of sin; that way, I could help others get free.

This book can best be described as my essay; it is the conclusion of what I learned while fighting with both the Jezebel and the Ahab spirits. Coupled with Volume Two of *Jezebellion*, this book will give you a thorough breakdown of Jezebel's character, her power, and what you'll need to defeat that wicked spirit once and for all.

Introduction

The Jezebel spirit is one of the most common and talked about spirits in the church today. We've heard a lot about this spirit and we've read a lot about it, but many of us are still ignorant to its ways. The reason for this is ... most of us are ignorant of Jezebel's intentions. Think of it this way. If your closest friend was distraught and had driven off in her car, you'd likely get in your car and go after her, right? That's because you know that it's not safe for her to be driving in the condition she's in. If you knew where she was heading, you'd be able to intercept her or, at minimum, follow her to ensure her safety. However, if you didn't know where she was going, it would be very difficult for you to intercept her. The same goes when dealing with the kingdom of darkness.

In the kingdom of darkness, there are many demonic spirits, each having its own unique function and assignment. Understanding a demon's function helps us to understand where that demon is heading or, better yet, what it intends to bring to pass in our lives. For example, if someone was wrestling with the spirit of lust, it wouldn't take a genius to figure out what that spirit's intentions were. If a woman is married to an adulterous man and that man wasn't at the place he told her he was heading, more than likely, she'd know where to find him. That's because after realizing his "condition," she started paying attention to where his "condition" led him. If a man was married to an alcoholic and his wife suddenly came up missing, he'd know to check the local bars. That's because after coming to terms with her "condition," he started paying attention to where her "condition" led her. As human beings, we are strategic, but sometimes, we come up with strategies to intercept one another, but we don't come up with strategies to intercept the enemy of our souls: Satan.

In this wisdom-packed book, you will learn how to identify the Jezebel spirit by learning how to identify its behaviors and masks. After you understand Jezebel's "condition," it'll be easier for you to know what her "condition" leads her to do.

In this book, I've also shared parts of my testimony and detailed how God delivered me from both the Jezebel and the Ahab spirit, so if you're looking to get set free, this book will teach you how to cast the devil out of your life. If you understand your "condition," you'll know where your "condition" is taking you. This will allow you to strategically intercept the enemy and take back everything he's stolen from you.

This book is a submarine of wisdom where you'll find yourself at the surface, getting the information you need before plunging into the depths of wisdom and revelation knowledge. You will come to understand how demons hide and how to cast them out of the darkness so that you can have the darkness cast out of you.

Before Getting Started

Be sure to familiarize yourself with the following words because you will see them being used throughout the book.

Ahab or ahab'ed: to cause to be like Ahab, to be made fearful. To be under the influence or control of Jezebel.

Jezebellic: like Jezebel, manipulative or controlling.

Jezebellion: a systematic and strategic plot designed to disrupt the order of God and expand the kingdom of darkness through the use of the Jezebel principality.

Additionally, I commonly reference Jezebel as "her" and "she," throughout this book, even though the Jezebel spirit can be in a man or a woman. I do this because the Jezebel spirit is more commonly found in women. At the same time, I want to make it easier for you, the reader, to understand each illustration that I give. I am not, however, promoting the idea that the Jezebel spirit can only be found in women, nor am I promoting the idea that the Ahab spirit can only be found in men.

CHAPTER 1

Jezebel and Ahab

J ezebel is the Anglicized transliteration of the Hebrew
אִיזֶבֶל ('Izevel/'Izavel). *The Oxford Guide to People &
Places of the Bible* states that the name is "best understood as meaning "Where is the Prince?," a ritual cry
from worship ceremonies in honor of Baal during peri-
ods of the year when the god was considered to be in
the underworld (Source: wikipedia.org).

Worshipers of Baal (a Canaanite deity) believed that
Baal was a fertility god. The Canaanites worshiped
many gods, with Baal being considered their supreme
god. The people of Phoenicia were either Canaanites or
they were a subgroup of the Canaanites. Phoenicia was
the land from which Jezebel (the woman) hailed from.

Biblical accounts of Jezebel show her to be a faithful
follower and worshiper of Baal. As a matter of fact, her
name "Jezebel" is believed to be a derivation of the

name "Baal." Like her father, Ethbaal, who was named after Baal, Jezebel was determined to spread the worship of Baal.

The Jezebel spirit is not the wicked queen of Israel in ghost-form. It is the wicked spirit that once possessed Jezebel herself. As a matter of fact, the Jezebel spirit roamed the earth thousands of years before Jezebel, the Phoenician princess, was born.

To understand the Jezebel spirit, we have to first understand the woman to whom that spirit derived its name. We must also understand the man to whom the Ahab spirit has derived its name. Lastly, we must understand the very principality that ruled Jezebel and ultimately came to rule God's people through Ahab.

First and foremost, the Jezebel spirit is not actually named Jezebel. We've come to identify that spirit as the Jezebel spirit because it was first identified when it operated in the infamous Jezebel of the Bible. What then is its name? The Bible never truly tells us its name, since the names of demons were blotted out from the Book of Life. They could not continue to use the names they once had while in Heaven. For example, Lucifer is now known as Satan. The name Lucifer means "morning star," but once he fell from Heaven, he was referred to as

Satan, which means "adversary."

Isaiah 14:12-20 (ESV): *How you are fallen from heaven, O Day Star, son of Dawn! How you are cut down to the ground, you who laid the nations low! You said in your heart, 'I will ascend to heaven; above the stars of God I will set my throne on high; I will sit on the mount of assembly in the far reaches of the north; I will ascend above the heights of the clouds; I will make myself like the Most High.' But you are brought down to Sheol, to the far reaches of the pit. Those who see you will stare at you and ponder over you: 'Is this the man who made the earth tremble, who shook kingdoms, who made the world like a desert and overthrew its cities, who did not let his prisoners go home?' All the kings of the nations lie in glory, each in his own tomb; but you are cast out, away from your grave, like a loathed branch, clothed with the slain, those pierced by the sword, who go down to the stones of the pit, like a dead body trampled underfoot. You will not be joined with them in burial, because you have destroyed your land, you have slain your people. "May the offspring of evildoers nevermore be named!"*

When Satan became God's adversary, he could no longer function under the name of Lucifer. He was renamed after his function. *This is the reason a deliverance minister can cast a demon out by substituting its function for its name.* Satan became God's adversary and as such, he was named Satan. For this reason, we refer to all dark powers as "Satan" because they are adversaries, but the overall devil himself is the ruler of the kingdom of darkness and he is not omnipresent, meaning, unlike God, he cannot be in all places at one time. That's why he employs demons to cover every inch of this earth ... wherever they can find legal entry.

How did demons get their names? Most demons got their names from the humans who *worship* or have *worshiped* them; their names were given to them in accordance with their functions or what people believed to be their powers. For example, Ishtar is the Mesopotamian East Semitic goddess of war, fertility, sex, and power. Ishtar falls under the Baal principality and is also known as Astarte, otherwise known as Ashtoreth. This deity assumes many names and each name is used by certain cultures.

Baal was the name of the god (principality) that was reverenced and worshiped by Phoenicia and some parts of Canaan. Jezebel was originally from Phoenicia. As a matter of fact, she was the daughter of Ethbaal, the king of Tyre. Tyre was an ancient Phoenician city. Ethbaal's named is translated to mean, "I am with Baal."

To understand demons, we must understand that the

kingdom of darkness operates very much like any other government. There are orders, ranks, and rules that demons must abide by. This helps them to operate in one accord. A principality is a governing spirit; it is a "prince" or a "principle demon." Principle demons (or principalities) are the highest ranking demonic officers that have been deployed against the human race. Principalities always have legions of demons under them. The highest ranking (human) officer in the United States government is the Commander in Chief, otherwise, known as the President of the United States. The President is followed by the Secretary of State and then the Deputy Secretary of Defense. After the Deputy Secretary of Defense, there are the Joint Chiefs of Staff, followed by the United States Congress. As the chain of command descends, it gets wider, whereas, the offices are more spread out. In other words, the United States government is nothing short of a pyramid. The same is true for demonic governments.

The principal demon usually covers a region, country, state, county, city, family and even some churches. Each principality's rank is dependent upon:
1. How many demons are under its rule.
2. How wicked the principal demon is. Some demons are more wicked than others (see Matthew 12:45).

3. How many principalities it is subject to. For example, a principality over the "Smith" bloodline may be considered a low-ranking principality because it is subject to the principality over the city, state and country in which the Smiths live. Believe it or not, demons respect order. They have to. They can't afford to be divided against themselves. To better understand this, think of the United States government. The mayor covers a city, but he (or she) is subject to the governor. The governor covers a state, but he (or she) is subject to the President of the United States.

The Baal principality has several functions and each function was dependent upon the region it was covering. For this reason, there were many Baals which included:

- Baal-Gad which means: lord of fortune.
- Baal-Zebub which means: lord of the flies.
- Baal-Peor which means: lord of the gap.
- Baal-Tamar which means: lord of the palms.
- Baal-Berith which means: lord of the covenant.

Baal, overall, was also known as:

- the god of fertility.
- husband, ruler, owner, bridegroom
- storm god

Jezebel was a Phoenician princess who worshiped the

overall Baal principality. In other words, she came from a pagan nation. She did not worship YAHWEH, the true and living God. She was just another pagan woman and the story should have ended there, but it didn't. Instead, the wicked Jezebel found herself as the chief ruler over God's people. She wasn't just the ruler, she was the chief ruler ... *just not on paper.* What this means is that even though her husband, Ahab, was king of Israel, Jezebel managed to usurp his authority and pretty much rule Israel by ruling Ahab. Ahab had the appearance of power but not the reality of it. He was not only controlled by Jezebel, but he was also controlled by Jezebel's father, Ethbaal. This is the way of the Jezebel spirit. This is very similar to the United States government itself.

Most Americans believe that the President of the United States has the most power, when this is not true. He has the greatest appearance of power, but not necessarily the reality of it. The President of the United States does have *some* power, but he is not the most powerful authority in the United States. The United States Constitution grants more power to Congress than it does to the President. Congress represents the people and can raise taxes, declare war, and can even impeach the President. The President cannot pass bills, but can veto the bills passed by the U.S. Congress. The President can also declare war and he has exclusive power over foreign policy. This means that the President does have *some* power, but does not possess the bulk of it. In other words, the President is pretty much the face of authority; he's similar to a man who owns a large company and has a large family but is controlled by his wife. In retrospect, his wife owns a large company and has a large family; he's just the face of authority. The same is true for Ahab.

Ahab was the seventh king of Israel. Of course, we know that the Israelites were God's people; they had been set aside by God. Nevertheless, when Ahab became king, he threatened to destroy Israel's relationship with God. How so? The book of Kings helps us to better understand Ahab's crime against God.

1 Kings 16:29-34 (ESV): *In the thirty-eighth year of Asa king of Judah, Ahab the son of Omri began to reign over Israel, and Ahab the son of Omri reigned over Israel in Samaria twenty-two years. And Ahab the son of Omri did evil in the sight of the Lord, more than all who were before him. And as if it had been a light thing for him to walk in the sins of Jeroboam the son of Nebat, he took for his wife Jezebel the daughter of Ethbaal king of the Sidonians, and went and served Baal and worshiped him. He erected an altar for Baal in the house of Baal, which he built in Samaria. And Ahab made an Asherah. Ahab did more to provoke the Lord, the God of Israel, to anger than all the kings of Israel who were before him. In his days*

Hiel of Bethel built Jericho. He laid its foundation at the cost of Abiram his firstborn, and set up its gates at the cost of his youngest son Segub, according to the word of the Lord, which he spoke by Joshua the son of Nun.

As we can see, Ahab did one of the things God commanded the Israelites to never do and that was ... they were to never intermarry with a pagan nation.

Deuteronomy 7:1-5: *When the Lord your God brings you into the land that you are entering to take possession of it, and clears away many nations before you, the Hittites, the Girgashites, the Amorites, the Canaanites, the Perizzites, the Hivites, and the Jebusites, seven nations more numerous and mightier than you, and when the Lord your God gives them over to you, and you defeat them, then you must devote them to complete destruction. You shall make no covenant with them and show no mercy to them. You shall not intermarry with them, giving your daughters to their sons or taking their daughters for your sons, for they would turn away your sons from following me, to serve other gods. Then the anger of the Lord would be kindled against you, and he would destroy you quickly. But thus shall you deal with them: you shall break down their altars and dash in pieces their pillars and chop down their Asherim and burn their carved images with fire.*

God had already granted victory to Israel over any pagan nation that dared to rise up against them. All they had to do was serve Him. Nevertheless, Israel had seen its fair share of wicked kings, but the Bible says that Ahab did the most wicked in the eyes of the Lord. Ahab intermarried with Phoenicia, taking Jezebel as not only his wife, but granting her the position of the queen of Israel. Why is this statement alarming? Israeli kings were known to have many wives and, of course, they would grant one wife the overall position of queen. For example, King David had many wives before Bathsheba, but he gave Bathsheba the position of queen. Israeli queens were rarely recognized unless they were noted to use some form of power against a king (see Jezebel, Athaliah, Vashti, Michal), they'd helped the people of God in some way or form (see Esther, Abigail) or they were the mothers of a king (see Azubah, Jecoliah, Nehushta).

Israeli queens were simply considered "the king's wives" ... nothing more, nothing less. It was very rare to hear of or hear from a queen. Nevertheless, Jezebel's power overshadowed her fearful husband's power. She wrote orders in Ahab's name (see 1 Kings 21:8), killed God's prophets (see 1 Kings 18:4), threatened Prophet Elijah (see 1 Kings 19:2) and was the very person Ahab turned to when he didn't get his way (see 1 Kings 21:6, 1 Kings 19:1). Even though she was queen of Israel, she operated in the power and authority of the king. She did this because:

1. She was a pagan woman who hated God and His prophets.
2. Ahab was under her father's rule.
3. Ahab was a passive and fearful man who loved the office of the king but did not want the responsibilities that came with it.

It was not uncommon for a king in those days to link his kingdom up with a larger kingdom. This was oftentimes done out of fear. Ahab likely feared Phoenicia and its power or he feared the power of the nations around him. Because of this, Ahab *literally* made a deal with the devil. He agreed to intermarry with Phoenicia and pretty much go under Phoenicia's rule in exchange for their protection. Now remember, God had already promised Israel protection and victory over its enemies, but Ahab did not trust God. He did not have faith, therefore, he was bound by the spirit of fear. His name is now synonymous with fear.

By intermarrying with Phoenicia, Ahab exchanged his true power for the appearance of power. He ended up marrying the evil Jezebel and she came and ruled in his place. He said and did nothing as she killed off the prophets of God. To please his wife, he helped to turn the people of God's hearts away from God and he set up worship centers for Baal in Israel. He began to despise God's prophets much like his wife. He loved false prophets and false prophecies, and he hated the truth. Ahab despised correction and anyone who dared to correct him. Nevertheless, he had some level of fear towards God. This is likely why he didn't have Micaiah killed when he prophesied the truth to him. He likely wanted Jezebel to do the dirty work and for that reason, he had Micaiah thrown in prison.

1 Kings 22:1-28 (NIV): *For three years there was no war between Aram and Israel. But in the third year Jehoshaphat king of Judah went down to see the king of Israel. The king of Israel had said to his officials, "Don't you know that Ramoth Gilead belongs to us and yet we are doing nothing to retake it from the king of Aram?"*

So he asked Jehoshaphat, "Will you go with me to fight against Ramoth Gilead?"

Jehoshaphat replied to the king of Israel, "I am as you are, my people as your people, my horses as your horses." But Jehoshaphat also said to the king of Israel, "First seek the counsel of the LORD."

So the king of Israel brought together the prophets— about four hundred men—and asked them, "Shall I go to war against Ramoth Gilead, or shall I refrain?"

"Go," they answered, "for the Lord will give it into the king's hand."

But Jehoshaphat asked, "Is there no longer a prophet of

the LORD here whom we can inquire of?"

The king of Israel answered Jehoshaphat, "There is still one prophet through whom we can inquire of the LORD, but I hate him because he never prophesies anything good about me, but always bad. He is Micaiah son of Imlah."

"The king should not say such a thing," Jehoshaphat replied.

So the king of Israel called one of his officials and said, "Bring Micaiah son of Imlah at once."

Dressed in their royal robes, the king of Israel and Jehoshaphat king of Judah were sitting on their thrones at the threshing floor by the entrance of the gate of Samaria, with all the prophets prophesying before them. Now Zedekiah son of Kenaanah had made iron horns and he declared, "This is what the LORD says: 'With these you will gore the Arameans until they are destroyed.'"

All the other prophets were prophesying the same thing. "Attack Ramoth Gilead and be victorious," they said, "for the LORD will give it into the king's hand."

The messenger who had gone to summon Micaiah said to him, "Look, the other prophets without exception are predicting success for the king. Let your word agree with theirs, and speak favorably."

But Micaiah said, "As surely as the LORD lives, I can tell him only what the LORD tells me."

When he arrived, the king asked him, "Micaiah, shall we go to war against Ramoth Gilead, or not?"

"Attack and be victorious," he answered, "for the Lord *will give it into the king's hand."*

The king said to him, "How many times must I make you swear to tell me nothing but the truth in the name of the Lord*?"*

Then Micaiah answered, "I saw all Israel scattered on the hills like sheep without a shepherd, and the Lord *said, 'These people have no master. Let each one go home in peace.'"*

The king of Israel said to Jehoshaphat, "Didn't I tell you that he never prophesies anything good about me, but only bad?"

Micaiah continued, "Therefore hear the word of the Lord*: I saw the* Lord *sitting on his throne with all the multitudes of heaven standing around him on his right and on his left. And the* Lord *said, 'Who will entice Ahab into attacking Ramoth Gilead and going to his death there?'*

"One suggested this, and another that. Finally, a spirit came forward, stood before the Lord *and said, 'I will entice him.'*

"'By what means?' the Lord *asked.*

"'I will go out and be a deceiving spirit in the mouths of all his prophets,' he said.

"'You will succeed in enticing him,' said the Lord*. 'Go and do it.'*

"So now the LORD *has put a deceiving spirit in the mouths of all these prophets of yours. The* LORD *has decreed disaster for you."*

Then Zedekiah son of Kenaanah went up and slapped Micaiah in the face. "Which way did the spirit from the LORD *go when he went from me to speak to you?" he asked.*

Micaiah replied, "You will find out on the day you go to hide in an inner room."

The king of Israel then ordered, "Take Micaiah and send him back to Amon the ruler of the city and to Joash the king's son and say, 'This is what the king says: Put this fellow in prison and give him nothing but bread and water until I return safely.'"

Micaiah declared, "If you ever return safely, the LORD *has not spoken through me." Then he added, "Mark my words, all you people!"*

To understand the Ahab spirit, we must first understand Ahab, the man. There are several points that we need to focus on in the aforementioned scripture and they are: **So he asked Jehoshaphat, "Will you go with me to fight against Ramoth Gilead?"**

Ahab, the Man: Jehoshaphat was a man of God; he had not departed from God and yet, Ahab sought him for counsel and assistance before rising up against Ramoth-Gilead. Additionally, Ahab had already made up his mind to go to war against Ramoth-Gilead before he sought the

15

prophets of Baal. That's why he asked Jehoshaphat first if he'd ally himself with him in war. It was after Jehoshaphat agreed that he sent for the prophets of Baal.

Ahab, the Spirit: Ahabs are oftentimes religious and they like to have at least one godly person in their midst. This gives them a sense of security and helps them to solidify the belief that they are still in God's good graces. They will seek godly counsel, all the while, seeking false prophets. Nevertheless, they will always prefer the advice and counsel of the false prophets over the true ones. At the same time, men and women infected with the Ahab spirit tend to make up their minds first and then they seek prophets to "confirm" what they've already determined in their hearts. This means they won't receive God's prophets because they don't want information; they want confirmation.

So the king of Israel brought together the prophets— about four hundred men—and asked them, "Shall I go to war against Ramoth Gilead, or shall I refrain?"

Ahab, the Man: Why did King Ahab need four hundred prophets to receive a word? The answer is simple. He was a man of doubt and he trusted in numbers.

Ahab, the Spirit: Ahabs tend to surround themselves with false prophets. This is one of the reasons it is so difficult to confront the Ahab spirit. Anytime a person confronts Ahab, he will not only turn to Jezebel for instructions, but he will access the many false prophets around him.

The messenger who had gone to summon Micaiah said to him, "Look, the other prophets without exception are predicting success for the king. Let your word agree with theirs, and speak favorably."

Ahab, the Man: The messenger who went to get the true prophet of God (Micaiah) told Micaiah to prophesy what the other prophets had prophesied. The messenger knew his master. Ahab didn't want to hear the truth; Ahab had already made up his mind and the messenger did not want to upset his king.

Ahab, the Spirit: Ahab spirits hate truth and are normally surrounded by people who are commonly referred as "yes-men." This means that the people around Ahabs don't tell them the truth; they tell them what they want to hear and then, they compel others to do the same.

When he arrived, the king asked him, "Micaiah, shall we go to war against Ramoth Gilead, or not?"
"Attack and be victorious," he answered, "for the LORD will give it into the king's hand."
The king said to him, "How many times must I make you swear to tell me nothing but the truth in the name of the LORD?"

Then Micaiah answered, "I saw all Israel scattered on the hills like sheep without a shepherd, and the LORD said, 'These people have no master. Let each one go home in peace.'"

Ahab, the Man: Ahab only inquired of Micaiah because Jehoshaphat told him to do so. Nevertheless, he already knew that Micaiah would not give him the same prophecy that his false prophets had given him. How so? Because false prophets normally say opposite of what God says. Micaiah decided to be sarcastic with him and say what he knew Ahab wanted to hear, but Ahab had already made up his mind concerning Micaiah. He simply wanted to give Micaiah a chance to either say what the prophets of Baal were saying or he wanted to utilize that opportunity to throw Micaiah in prison. Ahab did not want the truth, even though he'd summoned one of God's prophets.

Ahab, the Spirit: Ahabs don't consort with prophets to get the truth; they usually approach God's prophets when they feel pressured to do so or when they feel like they have enough power and authority within themselves to coerce the prophets of God to say what they want to hear. Regardless of what God's prophets say, an ahab'ed soul has already made up his or her mind regarding the messenger of God. For this reason, they look for fault in God's people and try to find ways to punish them for telling the truth.

The king of Israel said to Jehoshaphat, "Didn't I tell you that he never prophesies anything good about me, but only bad?"

Ahab, the Man: Before Ahab pronounced judgment over Micaiah (the prophet of God), he turned to Jehoshaphat, and launched his accusation against Micaiah. He did this for two reasons. For one, Jehoshaphat was a man of God. Ahab wanted to make sure that Jehoshaphat was not offended with him. Secondly, Jehoshaphat was the one who suggested that Ahab summon a prophet of God. This was Ahab's way of justifying his initial position of summoning the prophets of Baal. In other words, he was passive-aggressively accusing Jehoshaphat of not giving him wise counsel. Finally, Ahab was a prideful man. He felt entitled to good prophecies and he hated anyone who did not prophesy good to him.

Ahab, the Spirit: Ahabs tend to consort with godly men, but they do not receive nor do they respect their counsel. Ahabs want to believe that God is still with them, and even though they don't say it aloud, they want to believe that God serves them. For this reason, they will remove almost every godly person from their midst or ministry, but they will hold on to a few so that they can get their support. They don't want counsel from a true man or woman of God; they want support. They want the people of God to ally with them in their evil-doings and to back them up when they do wrong. Additionally,

Ahabs tend to be very passive-aggressive, whereas, they will indirectly accuse a true man or woman of God of giving them bad counsel, all the while, utilizing any opportunity they have to pronounce judgment on anyone sent to them by the true man or woman of God. That's because, in God's system, only a king could wage war against a king. Jehoshaphat could have confronted Ahab, but Micaiah had no authority to wage war against him. Ahab was simply making sure that the man who had the power and the authority to confront him was himself ahab'ed.

Jehoshaphat was like many leaders today. He saw that he'd allied himself with an evil man, but he either feared Jezebel or he simply wanted to ally himself with another king. Many leaders do the same. Some leaders fear the power and authority that other leaders *appear* to possess, so they ally themselves with those leaders. Others ally themselves with leaders they feel are of the same rank or higher than themselves and this is done out of selfish ambition.

Jezebel was a wicked woman who should have never been queen over God's people. Her marriage to Ahab was a clear depiction of what it means to be unequally yoked with an unbeliever ... especially when the believer is a man or woman to whom God has entrusted with power and authority over His people. The Jezebel spirit turned Ahab's heart away from God; that way, it could pervert and slaughter God's people. Jezebel's evil deeds have outlived her and her wickedness is only a small testament to the evil spirit that led her.

CHAPTER 2

Characteristics of the Jezebel Spirit

Every demonic spirit has what can best be described as a personality. These personalities or characteristics help deliverance ministries to identify the types of spirits they are confronting. For example, lust can oftentimes be seen in the eyes of a person and witnessed in the way they walk, talk, and the words they use. Anger can also be seen in a person's posture and heard in their words, even when they are not angry. Leviathan, which is the demon behind pride, can oftentimes be identified when a person is angry, scared, ashamed, feeling rejected, or that person feels entitled to something. The point is ... every demon has its own traits and the same is true for Jezebel.

There are many traits that help us to identify the Jezebel spirit and for a long time, many people thought that Jezebel was just a controlling, promiscuous woman who wore big hats and sat at the front of the church. Nevertheless, there's more to Jezebel and many have found out the hard way that if you are looking for Jezebel to come one way, she will come in another form. The Jezebel spirit is a demonic spirit and the person who has it is nothing but its host. It can be discerned, however, by that person's choices, words and behaviors.

Below are 44 characteristics and personalities of the Jezebel spirit.

1. **Jezebels feel the need to control people, things, and situations.** The most evident trait of the Jezebel spirit is its obsession with controlling others. Again, control can be both dominant or passive. They are oftentimes very emotional and do not like when they are not in control. This can be seen in their driving, heard in their words and witnessed in their body language.

2. **Jezebels hate authority and will challenge every form of authority that gets in their way.** When a Jezebel is in the workplace, she will seek to either gain the favor of her superiors or gain some information on her superiors that may possibly put their jobs or positions at risk. When a Jezebel is in a church environment, she will seek to win the favor of the church's pastor or his wife. This is done so she can gather information against the pastor and eventually control the members. When a Jezebel is confronted by an au-

thority figure such as a police officer, she will not admit to guilt, but will instead, write down the officer's badge number and make the officer aware of her connections. For example, a Jezebel will say, "I'm good friends with Mayor Smith and his wife and they'll be getting a call from me first thing in the morning."

3. **Jezebels are rebellious and think that the rules don't apply to them and for this reason, they hate rules.** Every time a Jezebel hires me to design something for her (or him), the Jezebel will not want to follow the rules posted on my website. This includes the small guidelines like filling out a short form to approve an order or reply to an email with the word "approved." Instead, they will respond the way they want to and I always have to tell them (oftentimes several times) that they must follow the posted rules. For example, instead of getting back an email that reads, "Approved," I'll get an email that says, "I really like the logo. Thank you!" When I contact the person and tell them that they have to write "Approved," they will oftentimes question the rules by saying something like, "I said I liked it. Why do I have to write "approved?'" The same goes when they go into a public building. They will almost always challenge the rules because the Jezebel

spirit is a ruling spirit.

4. **Jezebels are very self-absorbed**, even though they pretend and appear to be giving and nurturing. Jezebels are the faces of narcissism. Everything they do, say and plan is centered around themselves, even when they appear to be helping others. They tend to think that everyone is talking about them, plotting against them, or admiring them. They suffer from selfish ambition, self-pity, and self-worship. Everything they do and say is revolved around themselves and if you pay attention to every conversation they have, it will always lead back to themselves. They can talk for hours about themselves, but if you change the conversation, they'll either get off the phone with you or start talking to others in the background.

5. **Jezebels crave the worship of man.** They will always surround themselves with people who admire and praise them, but will intentionally and strategically avoid the people who see them as ordinary. They will tolerate successful or ambitious people who do not praise them, but this is only because Jezebel loves to use the names (signatures) of others to accomplish her agenda. Remember, Jezebel signed Ahab's name to the letters she sent out. Jezebels today love to be around powerful and successful people; that way,

they can use their names to accomplish their agendas.

6. **Jezebels hate the word "no" and will usually become infuriated when they hear it.** Anyone who has ever said "no" to Jezebel has felt her wrath. Jezebels will punish any and everyone who does not comply with their petitions or demands. This punishment can range from them publicly ignoring you while publicly acknowledging others, to them strategically persecuting you to others in an attempt to control how others see you.

7. **Jezebels love to collect evidence for blackmailing or exposing others.** They will record phone conversations, store emails, and hold on to anything they feel they can use to blackmail or expose their prey. Their friends aren't even exempt from their treacheries. For example, if a person who is friends with Jezebel were to tell Jezebel anything that can be seen as damning to that friend, Jezebel will record the conversation or remember pertinent details that she knows she can use should her friend attempt to escape her grasp. Beautiful Jezebels will even use themselves as bait and then "expose" any and everyone who bites the bait. For example, a beautiful Jezebel will know that a married co-worker is at-

tracted to her, but she will still go into his office and close the door or do things to lead him on. Once he bites the bait, she will threaten to expose him to the boss, his wife, or anyone she feels can ruin that man's career or marriage.

8. **Jezebels use flattery as a means of control.** They use flattery to get into the lives of others, and then, they use flattery to get what they want from the people they have successfully captured. They will even use flattery (not repentance) to hold on to the people who are attempting to leave their webs. So, instead of apologizing when they're wrong, they will often say things like, "I really treasure your friendship and if I have ever done anything wrong to you, it was not my intention. I think you are an amazing person and friend and I'd hate to lose you. I do think you are overreacting. Of all people, you should know me by now." This sounds apologetic, but it is not. They will never say, for example, "I was wrong for what I did to you. I prayed about it and God showed me that I was in error." Words like these are too hard for Jezebel to mouth, so instead, they choose flattery over repentance.

9. **Jezebels will use their titles to manipulate people into giving them what they want.** Jezebels are very ambitious, but their ambitions

are centered around achieving power and recognition. They will often say things like, "My name is Dr. Jane Doe and I am the CEO and Founder of Dr. Jane Doe Ministries. I'd like to order a cheeseburger ... no lettuce, a medium order of fries and a grape soda." In other words, Jezebels will give unsolicited information about themselves whenever they feel that information will serve to their benefit. This includes helping their daughters get on the cheerleading squad, attempting to talk themselves out of a traffic citation, or manipulating their way up the ranks at a local church.

10. **Jezebels use the names and titles of others to get people to give them what they want.** A common conversation you may hear Jezebel having is one where she tells another person about her connection or friendship with someone who outranks that person. This is an attempt to scare the person into submission. For example, let's say that a man with the Jezebel spirit walks into the DMV one day. Instead of standing in line, he walks up to the nearest window and asks for Lou (the manager) by name. If the manager is busy or isn't in the office, Jezebel will proceed to tell the person behind the window that he is in a hurry and that's why he asked for Lou. If the clerk tells him that he has to take a number like everyone

else, he will say something like, "I don't have time for this! Tell Lou that I said to give me a call asap! My name is Larry Williams! He knows who I am. I just spoke with him the other day. By the way, what's your name again?" This is a scare tactic designed to force the clerk to let him skip the line and do whatever he's come into the office to do. When the clerk talks to the manager, she will likely discover that Jezebel and the manager are not personally affiliated. Lou may say, for example, "I met the guy at a country club and anytime I see him, he starts talking to me about any and everything underneath the sun. He even tried to invite me to a cookout he was having, but I politely turned down his invitation." Jezebels like to be well-connected so they can control everyone they come in contact with.

11. **Jezebels are drawn to hurting people.** Pain and unforgiveness are two of the most effective doors for the Jezebel to enter in through, so anytime Jezebels hear about or come in contact with a hurting soul, they will offer their assistance to that soul. This is especially true if the hurting person is a person of influence or power. If the hurting soul is not a person of influence or power, Jezebels will still offer their assistance to them in an attempt to gain more followers for them-

selves.

12. **Jezebels use people as tools and will toss them away whenever they don't need them.** When Jezebel first meets a person, she will flood that person with praise and recognition, but once she has successfully soul tied herself to that person, she will toss them away until she needs them. You may go five months without hearing from Jezebel and then, all of a sudden, you'll get a call from her that sounds something like this: "Hey, how are you doing? How are your parents? Did they ever move out of that house? How are your kids? I was talking about little Benjamin the other day to a few of my friends. He is such a funny little boy. Well, you fell on my mind and I wanted to call to check in on you. How are you? Anyhow, the other reason I called is ... I have an event coming up and I need your help..." The nature of Jezebel's call was the event, but in an attempt to disguise herself as a friend, she started asking you questions about you and your family's well-being. Jezebel is simply taking you out of the tool shed because she needs to use you.

13. **Jezebels are masters of deflection.** Jezebels hate accountability and will never accept full responsibility for their wrongdoings. It is always someone else's fault. Their behaviors, according

to them, are nothing but the domino effects of someone else's words or choices. They will always redirect blame and guilt away from themselves and deflect them onto the people they are trying to manipulate. They are also good at "casting their reflection" onto others. What does this mean? If you are ever engaged in a battle with the Jezebel spirit, it will make anyone under its control believe that you are doing to them what they are actually doing to you. For example, a mother who's been controlling her married son will bewitch him into believing that his wife is trying to come between him and her when, in truth, she's the one who's trying to come between her son and his wife.

14. **Jezebels hate repentance and will avoid it at all costs.** You have to understand that a person with a Jezebel spirit will see repentance as a sign of weakness and a relinquishing of power. Jezebels seek to acquire power, not relinquish it. Additionally, Jezebels are very prideful and cannot stomach the taste of true repentance, so when confronted, they will often say things like, "I'm sorry that you got hurt over something so minute. If I had known that you were so sensitive, I wouldn't have said what I said!" In this, Jezebel isn't apologizing; instead, she's berating

the victim.

15. **Jezebels love to gather information about people so they can use that information to control them.** When Jezebels ask questions about your personal life or someone else's personal life, she's trying to sequester information to use as a means of control. This way, should you ever offend Jezebel or refuse to do something she's demanding that you do, she can threaten to "expose" you or she can sow discord between you and the person you spoke about.

16. **Jezebels like to sow seeds of discord.** One of the things you'll notice about Jezebels is that they will oftentimes sow discord between friends, co-workers, church members, family members, and so on. After that, they will act as the middlemen between the people who are at odds with one another. The reason for this is ... Jezebels don't work well on united fronts. They need division to function the way they want to function. They will pretend to understand your side of the story and then, go back to the other person and pretend to side with them. Nevertheless, the true story is ... Jezebel wants to keep the people divided and if they are to reconcile, she wants to be the person who brought them back together on her terms. This way, she has the power to separate or de-

stroy the relationship if it does not work to her benefit or if she feels her divisive ways are about to be exposed.

17. **Jezebels will hide behind religion when confronted.** Religious Jezebels are some of the craftiest Jezebels because they use religion and scriptures to justify their evil deeds or to hide their evil ways. When their wicked ways are exposed, Jezebels will often say things like, "God knows my heart" and "The devil is trying to divide us."

18. **Jezebels will walk in false humility when confronted, but their lack of repentance is too hard for them to hide.** One of the funniest scenarios to witness is a Jezebel attempting to be humble. The reason for this is ... their narcissism and pride won't allow them to do it, so they'll keep redirecting the blame to other people or masking their divisive ways as acts of nobility. They will apologize when exposed, but their apologies will often be laced with sarcasm, condescending tones, or overly dramatic attempts to cast themselves as the victim. Jezebels hate humility.

19. **When confronted with something they're doing, Jezebels will almost always point out your flaws.** For example, if you tell someone who

has a Jezebel spirit that you're tired of them complaining all the time, they may respond with something like, "Well, I'm sorry if *my* problems bother you! I'll keep them to myself from now on! I don't complain about your road rage when we're in traffic because I understand that you're just blowing off steam! But from now on, you don't have to worry about hearing *me* complain! I won't say a word!" The reason for this again is ... Jezebels hate true repentance and will use any and every method they can think of to avoid it.

20. **Jezebels like giving advice, but they hate receiving it.** Jezebel's pride makes it hard for her to be on the receiving end of ministry or counseling. The reason for this is ... Jezebel wants to be the most powerful, most intelligent, and most needed person in the room. Receiving counsel from another person requires humility ... something that Jezebel simply does not possess.

21. **Jezebels almost always threaten to "expose" the people who offend them.** This is true even if they have nothing to "expose." I have had two people to threaten to "expose" me when they had absolutely nothing on me to expose. Nevertheless, when a Jezebel does not get her way, she will mentally sift through every conversation you've had with her in an attempt to find some-

thing to regain control of you or the situation. One guy threatened to expose me because I rebuked him for abusing his wife and I would not tell his wife to return to him after he'd physically attacked her. He was very controlling towards his wife and I would not be as nonchalant about his violence as he was. I told him the truth, but he would not humble himself enough to receive it. So, when his wife left him and he couldn't reach her, he decided to provoke her to reach out to him. He sent me a long text message blaming me for the problems in his marriage and threatening to "expose" me. Nevertheless, because there was nothing to expose, his text message was laced with innuendos and assumptions.

22. **Jezebels will emotionally abuse their prey by ignoring or rejecting them whenever they don't do what Jezebel told them to do or expected them to do.** If Jezebel has access to your emotions, she will always use them against you when she does not get her way. This is especially true for familiar relationships between a parent and his or her child, siblings and marriage partners. A good example is what we commonly refer to as the "silent treatment." Instead of communicating her frustration with her husband, a wife decides to give him the "silent treatment" in an

attempt to change the atmosphere in the house to one where he cannot peacefully function. This is witchcraft and this is one of the "tools" that Jezebel uses to get her way. Sure, most couples are familiar with the "silent treatment," but most mature couples understand that it only works against the marriage and not for it.

23. **Jezebels will help out the people they are preying on and then brag about what they're doing for those people to others.** They will also remind their prey about all the things they've done for them. Let's say that you're struggling to come up with the money to pay your rent and Jezebel knows about this. If she can help, she will give or loan you the money for your rent and then, keep reminding you of what she's done for you when she wants something from you. Additionally, she'll tell others that she's paid your rent in an attempt to make herself look *needed*.

24. **Jezebels tend to defend unrighteousness more than righteousness.** They are the cool "go to" people who people seek out when they don't want to repent. Jezebels almost always come off as motherly (or fatherly), protective, understanding, and knowledgeable. This is because Jezebels love sin and hate true repentance. However, Jezebels will rarely defend authority figures; in-

stead, they'll defend anyone in conflict with an authority figure even when that person is clearly wrong.

25. **Jezebels have to be in leadership or on the set-up committee in everything they volunteer to do. If this doesn't work, they won't participate.** When I was younger and didn't know anything about demons or Jezebel, I knew a girl who would never show up at any party that I threw. Even though I didn't know anything about demons, I knew a lot about personality types. I knew that she was the type of person who would not participate in anything unless she was given a position of authority in whatever she was invited or asked to participate in. One day, I joked with a friend of mine about her not coming to any of my parties because she was not in control. So, to test my theory, the next time I planned a party, I told her that I needed someone to set it up for me. Sure enough, she came to the party and started taking charge of everything. I think we all know people like this. Every venue you go to, you will see them standing behind the desk or serving the food. They're not always charitable. Sometimes, you're witnessing a low-level Jezebel settling for any form of power that she can get or simply building her portfolio.

26. **Jezebels are often very casual regarding the topic of sex and will promote fornication and defend fornicators.** Demons tend to come in networks and the Jezebel spirit always comes with the spirit of sexual immorality (pornea). They are always "understanding" when the issue of sexual immorality is brought to the forefront. They will be the first to find you in a corner or secluded place and say things like, "Baby girl, don't let everyone know what you're doing; okay? Do your thing ... I understand, but you know how church folks are. They're the first ones to say something, but that's because they ain't happy! I know a few of their husbands who've been playing around. Shirley's husband has been hooking up with my best friend for the last six months! That's why she's the first person to say something when she hears that somebody is getting some ... it's because she ain't getting none! You hear me? Look, I'm not judging you. Do what you wanna do, but try not to be seen out in public. Come by my house later today and I'll give you the keys to my house in the next city over so when you want to get together with your man, y'all can meet up there." Jezebels tend to be drawn to people in sexual immorality and they will ferociously defend anyone caught in it.

27. **Jezebels will almost always accept the credit for every good thing that happens.** Jezebels want to appear needed and invaluable. For this reason, they will always draw near to people who are skillful and independent. For example, many of the Jezebels who order seals or logos from me will try to insert themselves into the design process. They may send me a sketch of what they want or they'll keep requesting changes to the designs. Now, I'm not saying that everyone who does this is a Jezebel, but what I am saying is that most Jezebels do this! They have to involve themselves in the process so they can take credit for the work. Once it's done, I'll often get emails or calls where the undelivered soul will say things like, "My vision came together well" or "I worked all night on that logo, but it finally came together." Ironically enough, when this happens, the design is inferior to my other design work because the process was controlled ... Jezebel had to ensure that her fingerprint was on the design so she could take credit for it!

28. **Jezebels will always try to control the direction and length of a conversation.** For this reason, Jezebels want to call you, but they will rarely answer your calls. This way, when Jezebel calls you, she can initiate the conversation by telling

you her reason for calling you and then, she can end the conversation when she feels it's not benefiting her in any way. For example, Jezebel will call you, talk about whatever it is that she wants to talk about and then, wait for your response. If you don't keep talking about her or if you change the direction of the conversation, Jezebel will pretend to be receiving another phone call or initiate a conversation with someone else in the background. She'll ignore you, end the phone call or place you on long holds so she can come back on the line and redirect the conversation back to herself or whatever it is that she wants to talk about.

29. **Passive, manipulative Jezebels will always cast themselves as victims.** Manipulative, soft-spoken Jezebels are oftentimes professional victims who always seem to need rescuing. Someone is always taking advantage of them, trying to control them or threatening to harm them. They will use their introverted nature and people's perceptions of them to deflect all wrongdoing away from themselves and onto whomever it is they are preying on. They are often master manipulators who successfully win over the sympathy of others; that is, until they can no longer hide behind their masks of meekness.

30. **Assertive, dominant Jezebels will always cast their victims as offenders.** When an aggressive Jezebel is confronted about something she's done to another person, she will always pretend to be the victim and redirect the blame to the person she's victimized. To validate her claim, she will oftentimes tell the person who's confronting her something the victim said about that person or someone affiliated with that person. What she says may be a lie or it may be something the victim actually said when he or she confided in Jezebel. If her prey is passive and soft-spoken, she will either lie on the person or expose that person's secrets. This is done to sow discord and to help Jezebel appear to be the victim or, at minimum, appear to be justified in her actions.

31. **When Jezebels are exposed in a city, company or church, they will leave that place and go somewhere where people do not know them.** This gives them the opportunity to start over and work towards regaining the power, recognition, and control they feel they are entitled to. Once a Jezebel is exposed, she becomes powerless against the people in a particular setting because the people will unify against her. Unity renders Jezebel powerless. This is why she sows discord between people.

32. **Jezebels do not like to blend into crowds.** They will often go out of their way to stand out. Many of them will reserve a seat for themselves at the front of the church, wear the most elaborate clothing, and sing or shout over others. They want to be noticed and they want to appear to be a cornerstone of any place that they frequent, be it church, work, or school. In church, flashy Jezebels will often wear the biggest hats or the most bejeweled outfits in an attempt to draw attention to themselves. Jezebels don't want just to be seen; they want to be recognized and admired.

33. **Jezebels love to say, "I told you so," or they'll tell endless stories about the people who didn't listen to them and ended up regretting that they hadn't.** I remember a woman who would always tell me stories about folks who didn't "listen" to her. The moral of each story was that everyone who did not listen to her found themselves wishing they had. She would also finish up her stories by telling me how those same people would find themselves needing her, but she would not avail herself to them. Her message wasn't difficult to translate. What she was saying was that any and everyone who does not follow her instructions will fail and when they do not

follow her instructions, she distances herself from them. This is their *punishment* for not doing what they were told to do. This was a passive-aggressive threat translated to mean, "I am the most needed and powerful person you'll ever know. Don't make the same mistake they made because once I turn my back on you, you will find that you need me, but I won't be here for you. This means that your life will be over and you will never have any form of success or happiness without me." Jezebels thrive on those moments when they are right because it gives them the opportunity to boast and to validate themselves as a needed authority figure.

34. **Jezebels love to use the spirit of confusion to gain control over a situation, especially if they are confronted.** Jezebels will talk incessantly and change the subject several times in an attempt to confuse anyone who confronts them. For example, let's say that you've confronted a religious Jezebel because you found out that she was the one who wrote a disparaging note to your pastor. Jezebel's response may be, "First off, you don't know what's going on, so I don't know why you are bringing this mess to me. I went to the store the other day and saw the pastor's wife and she's the one who told me that he was being

accused by one of the former members of falsifying documents. I didn't pay any attention to her because it's all foolishness to me, so I called my lawyer to see if he could help them in any way. My lawyer said that falsifying documents is a serious crime, but he's helped three other people get off when they were accused. He helped Ronald Smith to get off. Do you know Ronald Smith? Yeah, he was the one who was featured on that crime show and they tried to accuse him of the same thing. Church folks tried to destroy him, but he's doing good now. I don't know why folks do that. They will accuse you of just about everything. I forgot to ask you... how's your Dad? Is he okay? I saw him the other day and he was looking good. He told me about your new boyfriend." As you can see here, she has changed the subject several times because she is trying to weave her way out of a corner.

35. **Female Jezebels are often man-haters.** Female Jezebels can often be heard saying things like, "I told you that none of these men out here are any good!" They promote the idea that men are allergic to monogamy. They can often be found consoling hurting women and poisoning them with lies.

36. **Jezebels are compulsive liars who often lie for**

no apparent reason. Jezebels lie to accomplish their agenda. Jezebels lie to destroy the reputations, families, and careers of others. And sometimes, Jezebels are known to lie for no apparent reason at all. Remember that Jezebel is a false prophet, and every false prophet has the spirit of divination in addition to what is referred to as a lying spirit.

37. **Jezebels are very critical.** They want you to believe that nothing you do outside of them is good enough. The only time something is just right is if Jezebel did it own her own. Jezebels can often be heard saying things like, "I take one day off and everything is falling apart! I can't get a break! I have to shorten my vacation to go back to work, otherwise, the place is gonna fall apart." They want others to believe that they are the cornerstones and that no business, family, or ministry can survive without them. This is also the reason they like to be hands-on with everything. Criticism is Jezebel's way of building herself up by tearing down others.

38. **Jezebels are often clairvoyant.** Please understand that most Jezebels receive their "visions" and dreams through clairvoyance. This is why the Bible refers to them as false prophets. This is also why the Bible tells us to test the spirits (1

John 4:1).

39. **Jezebels love to surround themselves with beautiful and influential people.** Beauty, wealth, and power are all magnets that draw Jezebels. That's because beautiful, wealthy, and powerful people have the ability to influence large crowds. Jezebel will follow after anyone she feels can help her achieve her goal of gaining more power and more influence. Additionally, she likes to use beautiful, wealthy, and powerful people to validate herself to others and to gain the admiration of others.

40. **Jezebels hate true prophets and will try to bring them under their control or destroy their ministries.** True prophets have the ability to expose and destroy Jezebel and, for this reason, Jezebel hates true godly prophets. When Jezebels come in contact with true, godly prophets, they will first try to bring them under their control. They attempt this by giving the true prophets false prophecies or by trying to use their age, titles or seniority to bring the prophet into submission. For example, they tend to say things like, "I've been a member of this ministry for twelve years and I've served in ministry for thirty years. That means I was in ministry when you were but a twinkle in your father's eye." By

doing this, Jezebel is attempting to establish herself as the ruling authority over the younger prophet. If she cannot bring the prophet into submission, she will attempt to destroy the prophet by lying on him or her or by trying to sequester information about the prophet. That way, she can use that information to "expose" the prophet or control how others see the prophet.

41. **Jezebels hate prayer ... especially intercessory prayer.** They are oftentimes very religious and will request prayer for themselves, but they hate intercessory prayer. This is because intercessory prayer zaps them of their power and renders them powerless. They will often disrupt prayer by praying louder than everyone else. This is called hijacking. When my prayer line was new, I noticed that a few of the people on the line would hijack the prayers by talking over everyone else. They would break through all the voices of people praying by shouting over everyone and this actually worked. People would stop praying and start saying, "Amen." Of course, I had to put a stop to this behavior because I recognized that this was a jezebellic move. Jezebels hate prayer, especially when believers begin to pray in the Spirit. For this reason, they will disrupt prayers by praying over everyone or shouting out false

prophecies. They will also shout over the pastor while he's praying or speaking. This is to confuse the pastor and redirect everyone's attention to themselves.

42. **Jezebels will attempt to establish themselves as a parental figure to the pastor or whatever authorities they are subject to.** Anytime Jezebel goes into a church, for example, her goal is to take control of that church. But to do this, she has to bind the strongman or, better yet, the authority figure of that church ... namely, the pastor. For this reason, Jezebels will often go to churches where the pastors are younger than themselves; that way, they can use their age in an attempt to become a parental authority in the pastor's life. They'll do things like bring the pastor lunch, make sure that the pastor is eating right, and even keep people away from the pastor when they say he or she needs a break. This is Jezebel's attempt to become an influential and needed person in the pastor's life. By gaining control of the pastor, Jezebel is able to control the members through the pastor. She doesn't need to be in the pulpit to control the members.

43. **The people surrounding Jezebels are often afraid of correcting them or telling them "no."** The reason for this is that they've all witnessed

Jezebel's wrath either against themselves or against others. For this reason, Jezebels are usually surrounded by people who tell them what they want to hear and do what they want them to do.

44. **Some people who have the Jezebel spirit genuinely love God.** The truth is ... the Jezebel personality and the personality of the person bound by the Jezebel spirit are two separate personalities. However, when the Jezebel spirit enters a person, it uses their pain, rejection, and distrust of others to graft its personality into their personality. For this reason, some people who are delivered from the Jezebel spirit have to go through several deliverances, coupled with counseling so that they can be reintroduced to their own personalities and learn to live outside of Jezebel's demonic influence. Of course, there are people out there who love God and simply need deliverance; then again, there are some people who love their evil ways and do not want to be set free.

It goes without saying that these are just *some* of Jezebel's traits. As you'll come to see throughout this book, Jezebel is a very crafty spirit who is not limited to the personalities we've learned to identify her by. God told us to test the spirits and one thing we need to understand is that testing a spirit is the first part of engaging in effective warfare. For example, if I told you to go to the airport and pick up my good friend, Mary, my request is incomplete. If you agree to pick up Mary, you need to know how to identify Mary, otherwise, you'll go to the airport (get in position), but you won't know how to find Mary in the crowd (identify). You need to know more information about Mary or, at minimum, I should give you her surname; that way, you could stand at the exit gates and hold up a sign with her name on it. Therefore, when God told us to test the spirits, He was giving us a part of a message. To understand warfare, we must stick around long enough to hear or read the entire message. He also told us that we will know (identify) them (false prophets) by their fruits (Matthew 7:16). Of course, this is true for not just false prophets, but other demonic personalities.

CHAPTER 3

Characteristics of the Ahab Spirit

When discussing the Jezebel-Ahab duo, most people focus on Jezebel because the Jezebel spirit is the one who is the most aggressive. It is often believed to be dominant and controlling, while Ahab is oftentimes seen as its victim and this isn't always true. Because the Ahab spirit's role is often downplayed, that demon isn't collectively dealt with in the church. This leads to many believers performing a modern-day witch hunt, calling every dominant or extroverted female a Jezebel and attempting to shield every passive or introverted man. It is absolutely imperative that we, as the church, come to understand that while Jezebel is a wicked spirit that has to be bound, cast out, and sent into the abyss, the Ahab spirit is not a saint.

For example, anytime we witness a Jezebel-Ahab marriage where the wife is dominating her husband, we all collectively look upon the man in pity and wish that he'd be set free from his wife's fangs. This means that we often forget that what's operating in the man who's been ahab'ed by his wife is a demonic spirit and here's the truth ... he more than likely had that demon in him before he met her. That's why he was attracted to her and she was attracted to him. In other words, Ahab is not a kidnap victim or a victim at all. For this reason, the Ahab spirit must also be bound, cast out, and sent into the abyss. The church has to stop pitying demonic spirits and start casting them out. We can't choose to tolerate Ahab while casting out Jezebel; they both need to be cast out! Why is this? If a man is separated from his jezebellic wife, he will aggressively attempt to reconcile with her and he'll attack anyone who gets in his way. If she divorces him or passes away, he'll go and look for another Jezebel. The point is ... people with Ahab spirits need deliverance, not pity!

Below are 27 characteristics and personalities of the Ahab spirit.

1. **Ahabs are oftentimes passive-aggressive, but rarely ever passive:** Ahabs appear to be passive, but they are really passive-aggressive. Google defines "passive-aggressive" as: *of or denoting a type of behavior or personality characterized by indirect resistance to the demands of others and an avoidance of direct confrontation, as in procrastinating, pouting, or misplacing important*

materials. Whenever confronted, they will pretend to agree with you or understand your point, but once out of your presence, the ahab'ed soul will always run to Jezebel and tell her what you said or did. Even though they may not agree with you, in most cases, they won't tell you that; instead, they'll tell it to anyone they want to turn against you.

2. **Ahabs can sometimes be dominant and controlling:** Have you ever witnessed a bully being bullied? More than likely, you have. What this means is that the bully doesn't always act dominant and authoritative. His or her personality depends on the person he or she is in the presence of. The same is true for the Ahab personality. People with the Ahab spirit can be very passive and timid around dominant people, but when in the presence of passive people, they can be dominant and controlling. This means that we have underestimated Ahab. It is a chameleon spirit and just like its jezebellic counterpart, it can wear many masks. For example, Ahab (the man) was afraid of Elijah, but he did not fear Micaiah. As a matter of fact, he bullied Micaiah. That's because Elijah was confrontational, but Micaiah had to be summoned.

3. **Ahabs hate confrontation:** Again, Ahabs tend to

be passive-aggressive and will avoid confrontation at any cost. The reason for this is, just like Jezebel, a person with an Ahab spirit has trouble repenting or maintaining their repentance. They are sometimes docile, insecure, and afraid to voice their opinions. They are also afraid of backlash.

4. **Ahabs love to play the victim:** When Jehoshaphat asked Ahab if there was a prophet of the Lord available, he responded with, "There is yet one man by whom we may inquire of the Lord, Micaiah the son of Imlah, but I hate him, for he never prophesies good concerning me, but evil" (1 Kings 22:8 ESV). Ahab saw himself as a victim. Because Micaiah would not tell him what he wanted to hear, he hated him and did not want to summon him. People with Ahab spirits tend to play the victim whenever they've been offended, even when they are the ones who are clearly in error.

5. **Ahabs hate the truth:** Micaiah told Ahab the truth and, for this reason, he hated him. Elijah told Ahab the truth and, for this reason, he referred to him as his enemy. However, Ahab surrounded himself with Jezebel's false prophets and he showered them with luxury. Ahabs tend to surround themselves with liars and people

who do not hold them accountable for their sins. Remember, Ahab had Micaiah thrown in prison for telling him the truth.

6. **Ahabs tell their Jezebels everything:** When Naboth refused to give Ahab his vineyard, Ahab went back and told Jezebel. When Elijah confronted Ahab and killed the prophets of Baal, Ahab went back and told Jezebel. All too often, I'll come across a person who sympathizes with an Ahab they know. They'll reach out to me, trying to figure out what they can do to rescue the Ahab they know from the Jezebel they believe to be holding him (or her) captive. Of course, my advice is always to pray for both parties involved. Ahab is an adult and he's not the victim of a grown-man kidnapping. Howbeit, I've seen a few people attempt to rescue Ahab themselves. They'll catch him when he's away from his Jezebel and start telling him everything Jezebel has been doing behind his back. In their presence, Ahab appears to be humbled, thankful, and delivered. However, the moment he is out of their presence, he will tell Jezebel *everything* they said and then, offer to support whatever punishment Jezebel wants to inflict upon the person who ratted her out. Believe it or not, Ahab offers up family members, church members and friends as sac-

rifices to appease his Jezebel.

7. **Ahabs are strategic and will often have one true man or woman of God in their tool bag:** Ahabs tend to be very crafty and ambitious and for this reason, they always look for at least one or more people to act as a Jehoshaphat in their lives. Ahab likely believed that Jehoshaphat kept him connected to God. Jehoshaphat was too afraid to confront Ahab so Ahab ahab'ed Jehoshaphat. They will often look for people who are true men and women of God but are too afraid to tell them the truth, and they will use those people to validate themselves. They will appear to be receiving counsel from those people and even agreeing with the advice they've been given but, in truth, they more than likely won't be able to remember most of the advice they were given. That's because Ahabs don't want your advice; they want your allegiance. They will *tolerate* your advice if that's what it takes to get you to ally with them. Just like Jehoshaphat was nothing but a tool to Ahab, any person who allies himself or herself with Ahab is nothing but a tool of convenience.

8. **Ahabs hate responsibility:** With Ahab, Jezebels are oftentimes the decision-makers. In some cases, they even financially depend on their Jezebels

in exchange for their authority. They'll pretend to be the victim of their Jezebel's ferocious tempers, but if you question why they are sticking around and accepting the abuse, they'll often find some silly excuse to give you. In truth, they are co-dependent or fully dependent on the Jezebels they keep complaining about.

9. **Ahabs are known to repent, but their repentance is short-lived:** When Elijah confronted Ahab in Naboth's vineyard, he prophesied judgment to Ahab. After that, Ahab tore his clothes and fasted (1 Kings 21:7). However, once Ahab was back in the company of Jezebel, he returned to his wicked ways. I've met some Ahabs and Jezebels who can endure some impressionable fasts, but the one thing they all have in common is ... they avoid true repentance like the plague. If they can find someone to project the blame onto, they will deflect all attention away from themselves and cast it on that person. They will then cast themselves as the victims.

10. **Ahabs feel inadequate without their Jezebels:** If you've ever been around someone who has an Ahab spirit, you will notice that he or she has two conflicting personalities. When away from their Jezebels, they appear to be kind and understanding, but when in the presence of their Jezebels,

they are oftentimes overly confident, proud, and entitled (that is, unless Jezebel castrates them right in your face ... then, they'll go back to being royal eunuchs). The reason for this is ... they feel inadequate without their Jezebels. They don't like making decisions or calling the shots when Jezebel isn't around.

11. **Ahabs idolize their Jezebels while Jezebels idolize themselves:** Every time I've come across an Ahab, I've come across an idolater. Unbeknownst to the ahab'ed soul, he or she has made an idol out of Jezebel. I've seen men who were overly obsessed with demonically led women and ironically enough, those same men were loose and callous towards other women. I've seen women who were absolutely obsessed with and submissive to their jezebellic lovers, but those same women were once indifferent and controlling towards other men. The reason for this is once again, Jezebel is married to Ahab. If a man with an Ahab spirit romantically links himself to a woman who does not have the Jezebel spirit, he will try to make a Jezebel out of her or he will leave her for a Jezebel. The same happens with women. Demons are drawn to one another. At the same time, Jezebels aren't that into their Ahabs. You can often see a difference in their af-

fections toward one another. The ahab'ed person is often obsessed with his jezebellic lover, but the Jezebel almost always seems obsessed with herself (or himself), something else or someone else.

12. **Ahabs tend to surround themselves with Jezebel's friends and family and not their own:** Jezebels love to separate their Ahabs from their loved ones and Ahabs often feel happy to oblige their requests. I often tell the story of an uncle of mine who died when I was 24. He dealt mostly with his wife's family and we rarely ever saw him. His wife kept cheating on him and even had another man's baby while married to him, but he would not walk away from her. Eventually, she put him out of the house to move another man in, and within a week or two of this happening, the house he was living in caught fire while he was asleep. He died saving his son's life. All too often, Jezebels will separate Ahabs from their friends and families so they can do what they want to Ahab without any familial or familiar interference.

13. **Ahabs fund and fuel their Jezebels' attitudes and campaigns:** As the king of Israel, Ahab had the final say in what was acceptable and what was unacceptable. Ahab accepted Jezebel's ungodly ways by feeding and providing for the 450

prophets of Baal and 400 prophets of Asherah that Jezebel honored, while Jezebel set out to kill God's prophets. While this was happening, Obadiah hid 100 of God's prophets in two caves and fed them bread and water to keep them alive (1 Kings 18:13). The point is ... Jezebel's prophets were eating like kings and queens, while God's prophets were hiding in caves, eating bread and water. Ahabs always support their Jezebels, regardless of how wrong they are. That's why you'll notice that whenever a Jezebel is exposed, a flock of Ahabs, low-level Jezebels, and eunuchs will come out in support of her, even giving their money to her to help her in her time of need.

14. **Ahabs are covetous and depend on their Jezebels to give them what they want:** In most cases, Ahabs aren't ambitious because they tend to be dependent and suffer from entitlement complex. For example, if you come across a man who's been ahab'ed by his mother, you'll notice that despite his mother's complaints, he always manages to get what he wants. If he notices that his neighbor has spinning rims on his car, he will work diligently to convince his mother to buy rims for his car. If his mother does something for another family member, he'll get upset because he feels entitled to her money. Think about Ahab

and Naboth. Ahab felt entitled to Naboth's vineyard, so much so that he simply could not let it go. Instead, he laid on the bed pouting and trying to figure out how he could get his hands on Naboth's vineyard. He likely wasn't surprised when Jezebel offered to get it for him, nor did he attempt to stop her. He wanted that vineyard at any cost and unfortunately, Naboth paid for his choice to say "no" with his life. Ahabs can be those spoiled little rich kids who sit around waiting for their parents to pass away so they can get their hands on their wealth. I actually met an older guy like this once. He was more than 70 years old, but he looked every second of 90. He happened to be a perverted old man who lived down the street from me. He would always stop me when he saw me walking my dogs. He thought I was impressed with money, so one day, he told me that he was going to be rich once his mother passed away. He said she didn't have long to live. I couldn't believe what he was saying. I had never heard someone anxiously and excitedly await the death of their own mother. He was cold-hearted and dependent on his mother. I thought it was pretty funny that the Lord had kept her around for so long. Every time he thought she was about to go and be with the Lord, she'd come out of the hospital stronger and with a better report than before. She was over 90 years old.

15. **Ahabs are underhanded and cannot be true friends:** Jehoshaphat was likely swayed by Ahab's calm demeanor and his willingly to listen to Jehoshaphat. Like many people, Jehoshaphat thought he could reach Ahab and likely thought that he was "anointed" to win Ahab back for the Lord when, in truth, God was arranging for Ahab to fall. Ahab's cunning ways were displayed in the war against Ramoth-Gilead. First and foremost, he asked Jehoshaphat if he'd ally with him in a war that he was reluctant to seek godly counsel about. Ahabs tend to move in their own emotions and will cause their friends to sin against God with them *if allowed*. During the war, Ahab told Jehoshaphat that he was going to disguise himself, but he told Jehoshaphat to wear his royal clothing (Jehoshaphat was king of Judah). He knew that the soldiers would be looking for royal robes; they would be looking for Ahab. Ahab, like most kings, had more than likely studied his enemy's fighting style. He knew that the Syrians would be looking for the person wearing a royal robe. In other words, Ahab tried to set Jehoshaphat up to die in his place or be taken captive in his place. What's amazing to me is that Je-

hoshaphat was silly enough to go for it. Thankfully for Jehoshaphat, when he was being chased, the soldiers chasing him realized that he wasn't Ahab. People with Ahab spirits are very similar. They come off as kind and harmless, when they are actually underhanded and conniving.

16. **Ahabs are masters of manipulation:** As discussed in the previous pointer, Ahabs will set their loved ones up to save themselves. Make no mistake about it. An Ahab is only loyal to himself; everyone else is just a tool.

17. **Jezebels cannot and will not be "cast down off their walls" until the Ahab spirit has been bound up and "cast out":** Ahab is the one who had authority over Israel. He relinquished that authority by making an illegal and ungodly woman a legal queen over Israel. In order to destroy Jezebel, God had to first take away Ahab's authority. Since he was born a king, he would die a king, therefore, Ahab needed to die in order for Jezebel to become a trespasser. Without Ahab's authority, Jezebel was powerless, even as the queen. Therefore, in order for a person to get delivered from the Jezebel spirit, they must first want to be delivered and then, they must release the Ahabs whose power they're walking in. This means they have to repent, stop walking in

Ahab's authority and in most cases, separate themselves from the ahab'ed person. If they happen to be married to their Ahabs, the ahab'ed spouse needs to be delivered from the Ahab spirit and retake his or her authority. If the jezebellic spouse wants to be delivered, but the ahab'ed spouse doesn't, the jezebellic spouse must release the power they have over the Ahab, repent, and refuse to walk in the power and responsibility that God has delegated to Ahab.

18. **Sometimes, what we think is Ahab is actually Jezebel wearing one of her masks:** Remember, Jezebel sent out letters in Ahab's name. She does not mind pretending to be him if by doing so, she accomplishes her agenda. As I mentioned earlier, people tend to be merciful towards Ahabs and Jezebel knows this. I've witnessed a few passive Jezebels masquerading themselves as victims in an attempt to demean a person in authority. They will use people's perceptions of the Ahab spirit to garner sympathy for themselves. They will even claim to have had the Ahab spirit and have been the victims of ferocious, dominant Jezebels who were hell-bent on controlling them. However, if you actually test the spirit in them, you'd find that the authority figure simply rebuked them and because they did not want to repent, they

chose to to put on the masks of passivity and pass themselves off as victims.

19. **Ahabs do not want to be rescued, in most cases:** I've met plenty of Ahabs who've cried out for help but didn't truly want it. They will complain about the Jezebels in their lives, but I've discovered that when you are in leadership (especially ministry), this is often just a ploy to get in your life. I've had people to reach out to me who appeared to be desperate to get away from Jezebel. During the infancy of my ministry, I would give them my number, advise them, encourage them and then, sit by idly as they started referring to me as their "best friend" or friend. Months or years later, they wouldn't be any further away from Jezebel than they were when they'd met me. That's because all talks of being a victim was just to get me to open the door of my life to them. After that, I became what I now refer to as a "minister in their pockets" (Jehoshaphat) whereas, I became a person they could turn to whenever they were upset, confused, etc. What I've learned is that people like this do not want to be free; they want Jehoshaphats who'll tell them that it's okay for them to tolerate Jezebel. They want self-pity and a whole lot of attention (they'll usually call every day of the week, several

times a day). What I came to realize was the lesson in it was for me ... not them. I had to learn that a person who's not willing to help himself or herself is not a person who wants to be helped. This type of Ahab will enter a person's life, waste their time and then, the moment they are rebuked, they'll point fingers at the person who rebuked them and scream, "Jezebel!" At the end of it all, they'll be trying to attack your character, all the while, sticking around the Jezebels they once pretended they needed to be delivered from. This is crafty manipulation and it is common with the Ahab spirit. Most Ahabs don't want to be rescued; they want to be validated.

20. **Some Ahabs tend to be too nice:** As I mentioned earlier, it took me a long time to realize I was operating in the Ahab spirit because I'm not passive, nor am I shy. *(I did have a slight problem with shyness as a teenager, but I overcame it by confronting it.)* However, I did have a problem with being too nice. I would not confront people when they wronged me because I always found some way to blame myself for whatever they'd done, or I'd think I was overthinking something or overreacting. I became a prisoner of my own convictions and rules. With one friend, I kept silent about her ways because I felt like she was

too fragile to withstand a rebuke. Of course, she played right into my fears, so anytime I sounded like I was ready to rebuke her, she'd become apologetic, all the while, finding some type of way to share the blame with me or someone else. For example, she'd say something like, "I'm sorry. I guess I misunderstood you. It was the way *you* put it that made me think this was okay. I would never intentionally do anything to hurt you. I appreciate you as a person and I respect you, *but* you know, with me, you have to spell things out sometimes." She could never ever assume full responsibility, therefore, her repentance was always false and laced with blame. I've found that it is the misconceptions about the Ahab spirit that keep so many people from getting delivered from it. A person can be an extroverted Ahab, just as a person can be an introverted Jezebel. Sometimes, it's their own beliefs that hold them hostage. For example, I was taught to respect authority at a young age, and while this is great, sometimes, we can blur the lines between respect and letting folks walk all over us. When I worked in retail, a co-worker of mine told me about some adhesive tape the store had just placed on sale for ten cents. At that time, I was working as a phone operator. Even though I didn't need any tape (I was around 19 years old), a dime for a roll of tape was too good of a deal for me to overlook, so I excitedly talked about how I was going to go and get me some of that tape when I got a chance. My co-worker who, by the way, had come all the way out of her department to tell me about the tape, said to me, "I'll answer the phone for you while you go and get some tape for yourself. You better get it before it sells out. It's going pretty fast." I agreed and before I could rush off to the front of the store, that same co-worker stopped me and told me how many rolls of tape to get for her. I excitedly agreed and started towards the front of the store, but I was intercepted by the mother of one of my closest friends. Not only did she happen to work there, but she'd been around the corner and overheard our conversation. "Go back to your post!" she said to me, pointing towards my workstation. "Tiffany, you're too nice and sometimes, people take advantage of that. She could have gone and got her own tape. Why do you think she came all the way out of her department and made her way over here? Because she didn't want to risk losing her job and she knew you were too nice to say no! Go back to your station, Tiffany, and tell her to go get her own tape!" Of course, I suddenly realized that I was being taken advantage of, so I agreed with her, and walked back to my station. That's when I told the co-worker that I didn't need any tape and she had to go and get her own. I hadn't once considered that she was trying to get what she wanted, but protect her job, all the while, putting mine at risk for some ten cent tape. I couldn't grow out of the Ahab spirit; I had to be delivered from it and then, I had to mature in my God-given authority.

21. **Some Ahabs are legalistic souls who are prisoners to their own rules:** Again, this was the case with me. Saying "no" to an authority figure (older person, leader, police officer, pastor, etc.) was the equivalent of disrespecting them. That's what I believed. Now, there's nothing wrong with being respectful of authority; I plan to teach my kids to respect authority figures, but I had to redefine what respect meant to me. I've seen Jezebels dragging their Ahabs around by the hem of their legalism, meaning, the Ahabs had beliefs that allowed the Jezebels to take their authority away from them. For example, I've seen Jezebels volunteering the folks they've ahab'ed to run errands for other folks, not even asking them if they had the time or the gas to run those errands. The people under Jezebel's control would feel

obligated to do what they were told to do, all the while, trying to figure out where they were going to get some gas money from. They are slaves to the rules they've imposed upon themselves and again, sometimes, these folks aren't passive; they're just misinformed legalists.

22. **Ahabs are ticking time bombs:** Because Ahabs tend to bottle up their feelings and allow people to take advantage of them, they essentially become what we in the western world refer to as "ticking time bombs." This means that it's only a matter of time before every infraction they've suffered starts surfacing and they end up exploding at the people who've been taking advantage of them. Some are known to explode with words, while others are known to walk into buildings with high-powered weapons. Either way, a person who has been confined to fear is bound by the Jezebel spirit and if they do not speak out or no one comes to their defense, it's only a matter of time before they lash out.

23. **Ahabs accept their Jezebels' opinions as their own:** Have you ever been friends with a group of women, for example, and you disagreed with the Jezebel in that group? Consequentially, you and Jezebel stop talking and all of a sudden, you realize that everyone in that group is no longer

speaking to you? However, should you reconcile with Jezebel, everyone in the group suddenly starts speaking to you again? That's because Ahabs tend to forsake their own thoughts and take on the opinions of their Jezebels. An Ahab will never be loyal to anyone other than Jezebel. For example, an ahab'ed female would turn her back on her husband, children, pastor, life coach, and her dog if her jezebellic self-defense instructor managed to gain her respect. She'd challenge any and everyone who did not agree with her instructor. At the same time, I've seen lighter cases where, for example, an Ahab can have his own opinion and be sold out to his opinion. Nevertheless, once Jezebel shares her opinion with him and debunks his opinion as futile, he'll suddenly change his mind and accept Jezebel's point of view as his own. We often see this with U.S. Presidents, whereas, they'll boldly declare their positions regarding some policy or law, but once their jezebellic supporters threaten to cut off their allowances, they'll suddenly change their positions.

24. **Married Ahabs usually justify their adulteries by pointing out their wives' controlling or belligerent ways:** I have seen this many times where an Ahab will be the city whore while, for

example, his jezebellic wife is in and out of jail trying to fight women off him. Of course, Ahab is the one who bonds her out of jail, while the concerned police officers try to talk him into getting a restraining order. "That's my wife," he says while holding a bloody towel over his eye. "How can I get a restraining order against my own wife? All marriages have problems. We're no different." When the wife is let out of her cell, she signs the necessary paperwork and storms out of the police department with Ahab behind her, asking if she's okay, even though he's the one who's bleeding. The next time you see her, she'll be driving a new car because Ahab will work tirelessly or spend everything he has to get back in her good grace. One thing I've learned about Ahabs is that they tend to be irresponsible, so they choose marital partners who will assume the bulk of the responsibility in the marriage and will tolerate their adulterous ways. I once asked an Ahab why he was so determined to cheat on his wife, and he started pointing out the obvious: his wife was controlling, condescending, and rarely sober. However, anytime his wife threatened to divorce him or tried to leave him, he'd start whimpering like a motherless puppy and try to win her favor all over again.

25. **Married Ahabs usually leave disciplining the children to their Jezebels:** One thing that keeps a Jezebel being a Jezebel is anger, bitterness, and a sense of feeling unappreciated. That's why her marriage to Ahab is literally a marriage made in hell. Ahabs will usually be the fun parents, rarely (if ever) shelling out any discipline to their children, whereas, Jezebels are always left with the task of disciplining the children. An ahab'ed man, for example, can be heard whispering to his children, "Pick your toys up off the floor. You know how your mother is when she gets mad." That's because even as a parent, Ahab hates to assume responsibility or blame. They have to be the cool parents.

26. **Ahabs spin webs too:** Because people often think that Ahab is a "kidnap victim" who's under Jezebel's spell, it is not uncommon to see people trying to rescue grown men from grown women and vice versa. For example, an older man who's engaged to a woman with the Jezebel spirit may find himself constantly being introduced to other women by his well-intentioned children. Because he doesn't want to upset his children or because he likes the attention he's getting, he'll keep telling them every wrong thing his fiance does to him. Nevertheless, every time his children try to

convince him to leave his jezebellic lover or whenever they attempt to introduce him to someone else, he'll either rebuke his children, go on a date with the new woman and then dump her or he'll run back and tell Jezebel what his kids have done. Ahabs often like to be pitied and will take advantage of another person's sympathy for them. But make no mistake about it. Ahab is just as cunning as his wife, Jezebel, and he's not planning to leave her ... ever!

27. **Some Ahabs are nothing but Jezebels in training:** Just like every militant group, demons tend to follow ranks. A woman who has the Jezebel spirit may, for example, ahab her daughter. She will instill fear in her daughter and repeatedly hurt her until the daughter starts exhibiting jezebellic behaviors. She will utilize every hurt and failure in her daughter's life to sow lies and evil doctrines into her daughter's heart. So, for example, if a man breaks her daughter's heart, she may say things like, "I told you that men are no good! You didn't want to listen to me! You have to treat them the same way they treat you!" She will then proceed to take her daughter out to eat and buy a gift or two for her. What she's doing is grooming her Ahab to become a Jezebel. Eventually, the once fearful and passive daughter

will emerge from her shell as a low-level Jezebel ready to challenge her mother for territorial jurisdiction over their immediate or extended family. She is then confirmed as a Jezebel whenever she manages to ahab a person of authority. That's why ahabs and low-level Jezebels often reach out to leaders and complain about the Jezebels in their lives who they say are controlling or attempting to control them. They don't want to be free from Jezebel; they are simply trying to gain sympathy from the leader and eventually, bewitch and ahab that leader. The higher the rank of the person they manage to ahab, the more powerful they will become. Most leaders can attest to this: once they (the leaders) realize that the person does not truly want to be free, but is instead, focusing on their platforms, the leaders will start rebuking the Jezebel-in-training. When this happens, the ahab'ed soul or low-level Jezebel will accuse the leader of being a Jezebel, and then proceed to deal with the very person they once claimed they needed to be set free from. This is because they did not want freedom; they were simply Jezebels on training wheels.

Of course, there are many more traits and behaviors associated with the Ahab spirit that weren't listed. Ahab spirits are often tolerated when they need to be cast out, otherwise, they'll keep providing Jezebels with opportunities to have authority over God's people. Without Ahab, Jezebel is locked out. Without Ahab, Jezebel has no authority!

CHAPTER 4

Common Misconceptions

We often hear about the infamous Jezebel and Ahab spirits and it goes without saying that many people do not understand what the Jezebel spirit is. Many don't understand who Jezebel was in the Bible, and for this reason, referring to a woman as a "Jezebel" is the Christian equivalent of profanely referring to a woman as a "female dog."

Now, don't get me wrong, there are many, many Jezebels in and outside of the church, but because many people lack understanding, the Jezebel tag is now being overused in some instances and underused in others. Why is this a problem? It's a problem because the real Jezebel spirit is now slithering by unnoticed. At the same time, assuming that a not-so-friendly woman has a Jezebel spirit helps the enemy to better disguise that spirit. It also promotes the misconception that the Jezebel spirit is only found in controlling, bitter women —when this is not true. Most young people think that Jezebel is that seductive, middle-aged woman who dresses provocatively and sits at the front of the church in an attempt to seduce the pastor, but this isn't always true either. Of course, both of these women may very well have the Jezebel spirit, but their behaviors may be indicative of other demonic spirits or a demonic network where Jezebel is present but isn't necessarily the strongman. There are many demonic spirits roaming the earth and some of their personalities are so similar that we often confuse one for the other and that's why we need to be sensitive to the voice of the Holy Spirit.

Additionally, we must be aware of the wiles of the enemy. You'll notice that most women, when describing the Jezebel spirit, will try to disassociate themselves from it by only acknowledging the traits that they do not have. For example, young passive women may describe the Jezebel as being older, controlling, and bitter. Older, more dominant women may describe the Jezebel as being younger, manipulative, and seductive. I believe that women do this because the Jezebel tag is so commonly used that we are often afraid of being tagged with it. So what some women do is promote some truths about the Jezebel spirit, but not all of them. Men do the same. If a man has a Jezebel spirit, he will almost always promote the idea that the Jezebel spirit will only and can only inhabit women. If he is married to a woman who has that spirit, he will expose the traits that his wife does not have in an attempt to cover her and protect her from wearing that label; that is, if he wants to stay with her.

A few truths to consider include the following:

- Jezebels are not always dominant.
- Some Jezebels are very passive.
- Jezebel spirits are often found in men, even though they prefer women.
- Jezebels are not always sexually seductive.
- Your mate does matter after all.
- Every person bound by Jezebel has a story.

Jezebels are Not Always Dominant

Jezebels are always controlling, but they are not always dominant. How so? Please understand that dominance is only one of the components of control; manipulation is another component. Some of the most crafty Jezebels I've come in contact with were not dominant, but they were manipulative.

Some Jezebels are Passive

Imagine if you were Satan and you knew that Pastor Bill did not like dominant older women. Nevertheless, you were determined to get a Jezebel spirit inside of Bill's close network. What would you do? You'd send in a passive, sweet, younger woman who didn't mind working in the office of a servant! You'd send in an accommodating woman to pose as Pastor Bill's secretary! You'd send in a Jezebel who didn't fit Pastor Bill's definition of a Jezebel.

As I mentioned in the previous point, Jezebels are not always dominant. The goal of the Jezebel is to gain some form of control and believe it or not, manipulation is a form of control. Manipulation can be subtle and the person manipulating you can be soft-spoken and passive. For example, when the enemy saw how determined I was to not be dominated, he stopped sending dominant people after me. All of a sudden, I started meeting women who came off as meek, sweet and *seemingly* innocent. One thing each of them had in common was that they were determined to not only be by friend but to be my *best* friend. I used to wonder why most of the women I met would call me their *best friend* within a week of me meeting them. I didn't realize that the Jezebel spirit was basically staking claim to me. When the Lord began to deal with me regarding those women, it was hard for me to truly accept that I was hearing from God because they came off as meek. They did not fit *my definition* of the Jezebel personality. They would often turn to me for advice; they were rarely (if ever) dominant. But as time went on, I soon realized that I was being controlled in one way or another. In many cases, I was being bombarded with phone calls. They wanted to talk with me each and every day for hours at a time, several times a day. I didn't realize that my time was being controlled and I was being hindered from doing many of the things that God had assigned me to do. When I started taking my time back, what was in them started manifesting and one by one, those doors began to close!

Jezebel Spirits are Often Found in Men

Even though Jezebel spirits prefer to inhabit women, they will not and do not discriminate against men. Please understand that demons don't have genders and therefore, are not gender-specific. Demons like to pervert (twist or rearrange) whatever it is that God has set up. For this reason, they prefer to inhabit women because of the order God instituted in Ephesians 5:23. However, if a woman has a level of authority in Christ Jesus and that woman unequally yokes herself to a man, Jezebel will likely enter that man and begin to usurp the authority that God has given to that woman. A good example of this is if a woman has been called by God to the office of a prophet. If that woman were to marry a secular man, she would likely find herself lying next to Jezebel every night.

Jezebels are Not Always Sexually Seductive.

One of the biggest misconceptions about the Jezebel spirit is that a woman bound by it is going to be sexually seductive and this isn't always true. Jezebels are *always* seductive, but not always *sexually* seductive. Please understand that the word "seduce" is the root word of "seductive" and it means *to lead astray*. This means that not all Jezebels are scantily clad women wearing stilettos, long blonde wigs, and ruby red lipstick. Some Jezebels are not pretty or curvaceous enough to be sexually seductive, so they use fear, intimidation, and other forms of coercion to get what they want from others. At the same time, there are many, many Jezebels who are beautiful and curvaceous and they are not sexually seductive. Again, they will often use the powers of fear, intimidation, manipulation and other forms of coercion to get what they want.

Your Mate Does Matter After All
In the biblical text, we see the rise and fall of several kings and queens, but never the fall of the Kingdom of God. Israel has seen its fair share of wicked kings as well as its fair share of righteous kings, but in this study, we will discuss two kings and two queens. They are:

- King Xerxes versus King Ahab
- Queen Esther versus Queen Jezebel

King Xerxes was the king of the Persian Achaemenid Empire. He was not an Israelite man; instead, he was a pagan king. King Xerxes was married to Queen Vashti and as the story goes, he held a royal feast. On the seventh day of the feast, he summoned his wife, Vashti, to come and show herself to his guests. Vashti refused to come and this humiliated the king. He sought the advice of his counselors and a man named Memucan answered and told him to take Vashti's crown and give it to a woman who was nobler than herself. Some theologians use the term "divorced, " but in truth, a queen wasn't divorced in those times; they were deposed. The word "depose" means to remove from an office all of a sudden. Vashti would not be sent back to her father's house; she likely lived out the rest of her life in the castle, but she was reduced to less than a concubine. This means that she likely retained a room in the castle, but unlike the king's concubines, the king never slept with her again. She was still considered royalty, but she'd become a royal nothing with little to no powers. She would not be seen in the public eye, nor would she be fitted with the garments of a queen. In truth, this was probably worse than a divorce because she could not remarry and she had to sit from afar and watch another woman take her place.

The Bible never tells us what became of Queen Vashti, but more than likely, King Xerxes dealt with her in the very same manner that David dealt with his concubines after his son, Absalom, had sex with them.

2 Samuel 2:20 (ESV): *And David came to his house at*

Jerusalem. And the king took the ten concubines whom he had left to care for the house and put them in a house under guard and provided for them, but did not go in to them. So they were shut up until the day of their death, living as if in widowhood.

Again, queens weren't sent back to their fathers' houses, otherwise, they could be killed, plus, sending them away would have brought dishonor to the kings they'd once served. So, King Xerxes likely treated Queen Vashti as a widow and staged a few guards around whatever room or portion of the castle that she was to live out the rest of her life in.

King Xerxes saw Memucan's advice as good and he deposed Queen Vashti. He then held a feast in search for his new queen. This is how he met Esther who would eventually become his queen.

Esther was a Jew; she was not pagan. She worshiped the living God, YAHWEH. She had been raised by her uncle, Mordecai, and she was an obedient and submissive woman. She followed her uncle's advice and it led her to the castle, but it didn't necessarily get her on the throne. What got Esther on the throne was that she followed the advice of the king's eunuchs. You see, Esther wasn't a prideful woman who trusted in her own abilities or her beauty. She sought wise counsel and even though her beauty brought her before the king, it was her heart of submission that won him over.

Esther 2:12-16 (ESV): *Now when the turn came for each young woman to go in to King Ahasuerus, after being twelve months under the regulations for the women, since this was the regular period of their beautifying, six months with oil of myrrh and six months with spices and ointments for women— when the young woman went in to the king in this way, she was given whatever she desired to take with her from the harem to the king's palace. In the evening she would go in, and in the morning she would return to the second harem in custody of Shaashgaz, the king's eunuch, who was in charge of the concubines. She would not go in to the king again, unless the king delighted in her and she was summoned by name.When the turn came for Esther the daughter of Abihail the uncle of Mordecai, who had taken her as his own daughter, to go in to the king, she asked for nothing except what Hegai the king's eunuch, who had charge of the women, advised. Now Esther was winning favor in the eyes of all who saw her. And when Esther was taken to King Ahasuerus, into his royal palace, in the tenth month, which is the month of Tebeth, in the seventh year of his reign, the king loved Esther more than all the women, and she won grace and favor in his sight more than all the virgins, so that he set the royal crown on her head and made* *her queen instead of Vashti.*

Here it was that a Jewish woman of God was now married to a pagan king. Of course, God set this up to save His people because the Lord knew that a very wicked man was about to get into a position of authority. That man's name was Haman, and Haman likely had the infamous Jezebel spirit. Anytime Jezebel gets into a position of authority, that spirit seeks to destroy God's people and that's exactly what Haman did. You'll notice that right before Haman got into his new role as a vizier (king's adviser), God placed Esther in the office of a queen. Why was this? Because God is a God of order. To combat Haman, God needed to place a righteous person in an office greater than or equal to the office that Haman was in. So He chose Esther as queen because Esther had a heart of obedience.

When Haman got into position and realized that Mordecai and the other Jews would not bow to him when he passed by them, he used his position to the king to speak into the king's heart.
Esther 3:5-11 (ESV): *And when Haman saw that Mordecai did not bow down or pay homage to him, Haman was filled with fury. But he disdained to lay hands on Mordecai alone. So, as they had made known to him the people of Mordecai, Haman sought to destroy all the Jews, the*

people of Mordecai, throughout the whole kingdom of Ahasuerus. In the first month, which is the month of Nisan, in the twelfth year of King Ahasuerus, they cast Pur (that is, they cast lots) before Haman day after day; and they cast it month after month till the twelfth month, which is the month of Adar. Then Haman said to King Ahasuerus, "There is a certain people scattered abroad and dispersed among the peoples in all the provinces of your kingdom. Their laws are different from those of every other people, and they do not keep the king's laws, so that it is not to the king's profit to tolerate them. If it please the king, let it be decreed that they be destroyed, and I will pay 10,000 talents of silver into the hands of those who have charge of the king's business, that they may put it into the king's treasuries." So the king took his signet ring from his hand and gave it to Haman the Agagite, the son of Hammedatha, the enemy of the Jews. And the king said to Haman, "The money is given to you, the people also, to do with them as it seems good to you."

Haman did not realize that Queen Esther was a Jew because Mordecai told her before she'd married the king to keep her Jewish heritage a secret. Undoubtedly, this was a charge from the Lord and Mordecai likely didn't realize it at that time. So Haman set out to kill the Jews and he'd planned the very day that his evil deed was going to be administered. However, God had already placed someone else in a position greater than Haman's position who could also speak to the king and that was: the queen.

After hearing about Haman's wicked plans from her uncle Mordecai, Queen Esther's obedience was put to the test yet again. She was in the office of a queen; she did not have to take any orders from her uncle anymore, but she was a humble woman of God and her position as queen did not affect her position in God, meaning, she did not become prideful. *She was humble enough to hear wise counsel.* She listened to her uncle and went before the king. Because of her obedience, Haman's wicked plot was foiled and the Jews were saved. The point here is ... a woman of God managed to change the heart and mind of a pagan king through her obedience and her submission.

1 Peter 3:1-6 (ESV): *Likewise, wives, be subject to your own husbands, so that even if some do not obey the word, they may be won without a word by the conduct of their wives, when they see your respectful and pure conduct. Do not let your adorning be external—the braiding of hair and the putting on of gold jewelry, or the clothing you wear—but let your adorning be the hidden person of the heart with the imperishable beauty of a gentle and quiet spirit, which in God's sight is very precious. For this is how the holy women who hoped in God used to adorn* *themselves, by submitting to their own husbands, as Sarah obeyed Abraham, calling him lord. And you are her children, if you do good and do not fear anything that is frightening.*

Proverbs 11:14 (ESV): *Where there is no guidance, a people falls, but in an abundance of counselors there is safety.*

Let's compare this story with the story of King Ahab and Queen Jezebel. Ahab was a Jewish king; he *was* a man of God who married a wicked, pagan woman. Their relationship, however, was not put together by God. It likely came together because of Ahab's fear of Phoenicia and his lust for foreign things.

1 Kings 16:29-33 (ESV): *In the thirty-eighth year of Asa king of Judah, Ahab the son of Omri began to reign over Israel, and Ahab the son of Omri reigned over Israel in Samaria twenty-two years. And Ahab the son of Omri did evil in the sight of the Lord, more than all who were before him. And as if it had been a light thing for him to walk in the sins of Jeroboam the son of Nebat, he took for his wife Jezebel the daughter of Ethbaal king of the Sidonians, and went and served Baal and worshiped him. He erected an altar for Baal in the house of Baal, which he built in Samaria. And Ahab made an Asherah. Ahab did more to provoke the Lord, the God of Israel, to anger than all the kings of Israel who were before him.*

As we can see, Jezebel turned Ahab away from God and she led him to her gods (demons). She had him worshiping other deities. One thing we should note is ... a king always causes the rise or the fall of the kingdom in which he is leading. The Bible referred to Ahab as one of the most wicked kings to ever live. Why is this? Because Ahab did far worse than King Solomon did (remember, King Solomon married pagan women and they turned his heart from God). Ahab allowed his wife to start slaughtering God's prophets and he despised the truth.

The point is ... the queen matters. If you're a man looking to get married, understand that the queen matters. If you're a single woman hoping to someday get married, understand that the queen matters. You can be a wicked queen or you can be a righteous one, but you do matter.

The person who gets on the throne of your heart plays a very important role in your story. Anytime a woman of God goes after an ungodly, secular man, it is because she is practicing spiritual pedophilia and she is being influenced by the Jezebel or the Ahab spirit. Anytime a man of God goes after an ungodly, secular woman, it is because he is practicing spiritual pedophilia and he is being led by the Jezebel or the Ahab spirit. Choosing a spouse is not only important to our lives; it is important to the people we are called to lead and follow, just as it is important to our forever destinations (heaven or hell).

Anytime I've come across a man married to a woman who has the Jezebel spirit, I've noticed how drained he appears. That's because he has to fight against his enemy, guard himself against his enemy and then, go to bed with her. In the bedroom, he gives her what's left of his strength.

Proverbs 31:3 (ESV): *Do not give your strength to women, your ways to those who destroy kings.*

This means that his warfare is no longer just internal, but it now has two legs and is wearing his last name (signature of approval, authorization). In other words, he's not just double-minded and unstable, but he's being forced to live a double life. However, it was his lust and his idolatrous ways that led him into Jezebel's snare, so in order for him to get delivered from Jezebel, he has to be delivered from whatever it was that led him to Jezebel.

Anytime I've come across a woman married to a man who has the Jezebel spirit, I've noticed how dark and hollow her eyes look. Her husband has managed to erase almost every sign of life from her eyes, and all she can seem to see is the slow death of her marriage taking

place right before her. When she asks for help from leaders, she begs for someone to cast the devils out of her
husband, not realizing that she needs the most deliverance. How so? It was her idolatry that empowered
Jezebel in the first place. Nevertheless, even when
standing directly in front of her, such a woman is hard to
reach. To get delivered from Jezebel, she has to find out
what led her to Jezebel and get delivered from it because deliverance comes in layers. In most cases, the
woman in question is a prophetess. This is the reason
Satan sent Jezebel after her. Remember, Jezebel hates
prophets. To imagine her plight, imagine what would
have happened if Elijah had married Jezebel and had to
wake up to her everyday.

Again, many people don't think who they choose to marry is important, but I can honestly say that if we were allowed (in our living states) to speak with King Xerxes
and King Ahab, they'd beg to differ. When we get married, our life's choices aren't just ours anymore; we partner up with another person and we join our visions with
theirs.

Every Person Bound by Jezebel has a Story
How did she get like that? I've asked that question many
times upon meeting some of the people I've met. My
company puts me in direct contact with new customers

every day and I've met some of the friendliest souls, just as I've met some of the nastiest ones.

I remember one customer in particular. Over the phone, she was friendly and respectful, but whenever she would email me, her emails would be very condescending and rude. It felt like I was dealing with two *completely* different people, after all, I was definitely dealing with two *completely* different personalities. When I'd receive a not-so-friendly email from her, I'd call and the personality that answered the phone was nice; she was *very* nice. After speaking with her, I would feel assured that whatever questions or problems she had were put to rest, but another condescending email would diffuse that theory. I'd call her and again, the personality that answered would not be the same one that I'd just gotten an email from. I wanted to move forward with the order, but there was always some sort of hold-up. She wouldn't send me everything I needed to complete the order and it became clear to me that we were in the middle of a dance ... a tango of sorts. She didn't seem to be too interested in getting her project completed; she wanted to talk and email back and forth. She'd even told me that she was coming to my city and wanted to hang out with me. Of course, I screamed "no" in my head. I don't get personally involved with my customers. Nevertheless, I said, "Sounds good," hoping that the personality on the line would relay to the other personality that I was kind and easy to work with. I knew there was *no way* I was going to be hanging out with that woman but, at the same time, I was starting to feel anxious. I desperately wanted to finish that order because I had been feeling tension in my shoulders and getting slight headaches ever since I'd started working with her. At the same time, I'd worked with her before. Not *her* per se, but Jezebel. I've worked with the Jezebel spirit on many occasions and I recognized her movements. The project was secondary; her entire focus was on creating a friendship (soul tie) with me. Needless to say, it was pretty clear to her that I simply wanted to finish the transaction. She kept trying to deal with me personally, but I kept responding to her professionally, and that only seemed to agitate her all the more. Nevertheless, that agitation would never be evident over the phone. I knew what needed to be done. I needed to refund her order because it was turning into a time-consuming, emotional ordeal where nothing was getting done but a lot was being said. I reminded myself time and time again to remain professional, but after I'd received a few emails, my little motivational speeches to self weren't working anymore. I then began praying to the Lord be-cause I'd exhausted everything I knew to do other than to refund her. I normally have to refund one or two cus-tomers a year, and that's not bad, given that I work with hundreds of ministries each year. Every time I refund a customer, I ban that customer, so it goes without saying that I like to exhaust every avenue possible before going to that extreme. Nevertheless, the Lord kept telling me to wait. I thought that He was going to deal with her heart, but He had something else in mind. A few days later, I received a lengthy, condescending email from the customer demanding a refund. I had just woken up and was about to start my day. I'd checked my iPad, and that's when I saw the email. When I received the email, I was overcome with excitement. I rushed downstairs, hoping that I'd get to my work computer before she changed her mind. I had never been so happy to refund a customer in my life.

How did she get like that? The question sprung up in my heart again and that's when I started seeing a vision. I saw a woman in what looked like a very small and dark room. The room was so small that it reminded me of a tiny prison cell, but it didn't have bars. The door to the room opened and the woman was crying. That's when the door shut. The door opened and closed several times and the last time it opened, the woman was no longer crying. She looked like the same woman, but there was something different about her eyes. She looked up at the figure who'd opened the door and she was then allowed to come out of that room. There was

Common Misconceptions

an unmistakable evil in her eyes. It appeared that she'd been locked in that room until every trace of love and humanity had left her soul. The entire ordeal reminded me of someone checking their food while it was in the microwave until it was just the right temperature to pull out.

Needless to say, as much as I wanted to be angry with her, I couldn't. Don't get me wrong, I was frustrated with the entire ordeal and I had gotten angry with her a few times, but I kept reminding myself that there was a reason she behaved the way she did. Everyone has a story and even though our pasts don't justify us being rude to others, the fact remains that hurt people hurt people.

What I've learned is that many Jezebels are created in pain. They are hurt time and time again until the darkness that surrounds them becomes the darkness that fills them. The Jezebel spirit attacks both men and women in their youth, and it normally uses people in authority to carry out its wicked deeds against them. The reason for this is the Jezebel spirit wants its hosts to fear or hate authority figures. It wants them to fear not being in control; that way, they will always try to usurp the authority of any and everyone who has authority.

There are many misconceptions about the Jezebel spirit.

98

The truth is that the devil loves to promote these common misconceptions and misunderstandings regarding the Jezebel spirit; that way, the demon itself can slither by undetected. As we continue on in this manual, we will further discuss and elaborate on the aforementioned pointers as well as other common misunderstandings regarding both the Jezebel and the Ahab spirits.

CHAPTER 5

Understanding Demonic Hierarchy

We are definitely living in a time where the Jezebel spirit is being praised and promoted. This is because the more intelligent mankind gets, the more mankind rebels against the Lord. Because of all the advances in technology, many people are starting to believe that they don't need YAHWEH and sadly enough, this mentality has even bled over into in some churches. Nowadays, we see an influx in sin and sin acceptance, just as we see an influx in believers defending sin. This is because the enemy has managed to get this generation to misunderstand and attempt to redefine the word "love." Nowadays, people tend to over-emotionalize love and accept what God (who is Love, by the way) has rejected.

What is love? The Bible tells us that love is not a "what" but a "who." God is love and He has established what He loves and what He hates.

Proverbs 6:16-19 (ESV): *There are six things that the Lord hates, seven that are an abomination to him:*

101

haughty eyes, a lying tongue, and hands that shed inno-cent blood, a heart that devises wicked plans, feet that make haste to run to evil, a false witness who breathes out lies, and one who sows discord among brothers.

Malachi 2:16 (ESV): *"For I hate divorce!" says the LORD, the God of Israel. "To divorce your wife is to overwhelm her with cruelty," says the LORD of Heaven's Armies. "So guard your heart; do not be unfaithful to your wife."*

In addition to detailing what He hates, God also tells us throughout the Scriptures what He says is an abomination to Him. The word "abomination" goes much further than the word hate. It means to be abhorrent, repugnant, and unacceptable. For example, the scriptures below tell us what God sees as "abominable."

Proverbs 11:1 (ESV): *A false balance is an abomination to the LORD, but a just weight is his delight.*

Proverbs 11:20 (KJV): *They that are of a perverse heart are abomination to the LORD: but such as are upright in their way are his delight.*

Proverbs 12:22 (ESV): *Lying lips are an abomination to the LORD, but those who act faithfully are his delight.*

Proverbs 15:8 (ESV): *The sacrifice of the wicked is an abomination to the LORD, but the prayer of the upright is acceptable to him.*

Proverbs 15:26 (ESV): *The thoughts of the wicked are an abomination to the LORD, but gracious words are* *pure.*

Proverbs 16:5 (ESV): *Everyone who is arrogant in heart is an abomination to the LORD; be assured, he will not go unpunished.*

Proverbs 17:15 (ESV): *He who justifies the wicked and he who condemns the righteous are both alike an abomination to the LORD.*

Proverbs 21:27 (ESV): *The sacrifice of the wicked is an abomination; how much more when he brings it with evil intent.*

Luke 16:15 (ESV): *And he said to them, "You are those who justify yourselves before men, but God knows your hearts. For what is exalted among men is an abomination in the sight of God.*

Satan's agenda is to cause people to love the very things that God hates ... even the things that He finds abominable. The reason for this is that the enemy wants to take over this world; he still wants to be like God. He still wants to be God. For this reason, he has released one of his most wicked principalities and that principality is: the Jezebel spirit.

First and foremost, what is the difference between a simple demon versus a principality? We all know that a demon is a fallen angel; it is an angel of darkness, whereas, God is a God of light. It is believed that when

Satan was evicted from Heaven, a third of Heaven's angels were "cast out" of Heaven with him. Because God is light, those angels could not retain light, so they became the angels of darkness that we commonly refer to as demons or devils. When Adam fell into sin, God cast him out of the Garden of Eden along with his wife, Eve. That's because Eden was a holy place, but Adam and Eve were no longer holy. This meant that they could no longer dwell in the Holy Place where the light of God was. Jesus Christ came and reconciled us to the Father. He basically cut the lights back on in our lives, thus, making it illegal for darkness to dwell in us.

2 Corinthians 6:14 (ESV): *Do not be unequally yoked with unbelievers. For what partnership has righteousness with lawlessness? Or what fellowship has light with darkness?*

Matthew 27:50-54 (ESV): *And Jesus cried out again with a loud voice and yielded up his spirit. And behold, the curtain of the temple was torn in two, from top to bottom. And the earth shook, and the rocks were split. The tombs also were opened. And many bodies of the saints who had fallen asleep were raised, and coming out of the tombs after his resurrection they went into the holy city and appeared to many. When the centurion and those who were with him, keeping watch over Jesus, saw the earthquake and what took place, they were filled with awe and said, "Truly this was the Son of God!"*

John 1:5 (ESV): *The light shines in the darkness, and the darkness has not overcome it.*

Therefore, a demon is but a fallen angel or an angel without Christ. Light represents life, whereas, darkness is synonymous with death.

A principality, on the other hand, is a demonic authority or high-ranking demon. It is the "principle" demon or the "prince." This means that it runs like a kingdom, whereas, there is a prince and there are many officers under that prince. Of course, in the kingdom of darkness, Satan operates as a king. Jezebel is considered a "prince" or "principle" demon. Since demons don't have genders, we often refer to them using masculine verbiage (because God refers to them this way), however, when speaking of the Jezebel spirit, it is more common for us to refer to it using feminine verbiage. This is because Jezebel, in the Bible, was a woman; she was a princess who worshiped the Baal principality, better known as the Baal spirit.

Principalities normally cover countries, regions, states, provinces, cities, counties, neighborhoods and governments as a whole. They even cover families and manifest in what we call "generational curses." A principality over a family will deploy familiar spirits to bring a series of conditions and mindsets within that family. Of course, there are some principalities that are subject to other principalities. For example, a principality over a particular city is subject to the principality over that entire state. A principality over a state is subject to a principality over a region. A principality over a region is subject to a principality over a country.

The Jezebel spirit is a principality, but it is subject to the Baal principality. Additionally, there are high-ranking Jezebel spirits, just as there are low-ranking Jezebel spirits or principalities. A low-ranking Jezebel can be the family witch ... someone who has managed to rob a family of their authority. It can be that aunt who has garnered some form of success and now, the family depends on her for financial provision. To get her money, of course, means to receive her advice, instructions or better yet, her demands. A high-ranking Jezebel will be found in higher places such as governmental offices, large churches, mass media or any place where it can influence a greater number of people. Each Jezebel spirit works with its superior to accomplish a common agenda and, of course, that agenda is to rid the world of the light so that it can be ruled by darkness.

Satan understands authority and unity. For this reason, he works around the clock to garner followers for himself by catering to the death in mankind. The death in a believer is that area that the believer has not submitted to God. It is the place where lust, covetousness, pride and envy resides. This is the place that gives the enemy access to believers. For this reason, many believers find themselves being trespassed upon by demonic spirits. Understand this: demons cannot reside where there is light, so they access believers in the dark areas of their hearts. This is why after casting demonic spirits out a believer, most deliverance ministers will tell the newly delivered soul to ask the Holy Spirit to come and dwell in those areas that they just received deliverance in. In other words, what the believer is told to do is to let the light of God reside in that portion of the believer's heart; that way, the enemy cannot return. This means that in order for the believer to maintain his or her deliverance, that believer must sincerely repent or turn away from the darkness that gave the enemy access to him or her and then, ask the Holy Spirit to come and reside in that area of his or her heart.

Matthew 12:43-45 (ESV): *When the unclean spirit has gone out of a person, it passes through waterless places seeking rest, but finds none. Then it says, 'I will return to my house from which I came.' And when it comes, it finds the house empty, swept, and put in order. Then it goes and brings with it seven other spirits more evil than itself, and they enter and dwell there, and the last state of that* *person is worse than the first. So also will it be with this evil generation."*

Just like the Kingdom of God and the kingdom of man, the kingdom of darkness has hierarchies and the higher on the pyramid an agent is, the more power that agent possesses. For example, the governor of a state has more power than a mayor of a city. The same is true in demonic governments. That's why some demons are more evil than others and some are harder to cast out than others. For example, a ruler over a county is far more wicked than a familiar spirit that rules over a particular family.

Ephesians 6:12 (ESV): *For we do not wrestle against flesh and blood, but against the rulers, against the authorities, against the cosmic powers over this present darkness, against the spiritual forces of evil in the heavenly places.*

When dealing with the Jezebel spirit, we are dealing with a "ruler," and anywhere you find a principality or ruler, you will find a host of demonic spirits under that ruler. That's because demons like to work in networks. Under the Jezebel principality, you'll always find the Ahab spirit, the spirit of fear, controlling spirits, seducing spirits, lust, whoredom spirits, idolatry, pride, spirits of mind control, antichrist spirits, spirits of murder, premature death, rejection, abandonment, covetousness, the spirit of divination, spirits of witchcraft, religious spirits, lying spirits, spirits of unbelief, spirits of seduction, and much more. Each demonic spirit has a function, a rank and an assignment.

Some of Jezebel's most used spirits, especially when it's trying to gain access to a person, are seducing spirits, the spirit of fear, witchcraft, divination and doubt. For example, Jezebel's most effective weapon is getting a believer to doubt God. A man with a Jezebel spirit may ask someone he's trying to indoctrinate, "Are you sure God told you that?" His demonic assignment is to sow seeds of discouragement and disbelief; his goal is to get the listener to doubt God. The enemy wants to unlock an area of the listener where he cannot access, so if the man believes God, but does not possess the knowledge (light of truth) he needs to stay grounded, the enemy will attack or darken that area of his belief system. The enemy will then attempt to get him to doubt God so that he can introduce to him the doctrines of demons. This is why we see so many demonic religions suddenly springing up and gaining momentum. If he is successful, the new recruit's belief system or heart has just been infiltrated and that area of his belief system will be rendered dark. This allows demonic spirits to come and inhabit the man in that area of his heart and, of course, demons don't like to be restricted, so they'll continue to challenge every godly belief with a question: "Did God really say that?" or "Are you sure you heard from God?" Their goal is to *sear* the man's conscience.

1 Timothy 4:1-3 (ESV): *Now the Spirit expressly says that in later times some will depart from the faith by devoting themselves to deceitful spirits and teachings of demons, through the insincerity of liars whose consciences are seared, who forbid marriage and require abstinence from foods that God created to be received with thanksgiving by those who believe and know the truth.*

Merriam-Webster defines the word "sear" as: *to cause withering or drying.* What is withered and dry? Things that are dead, of course. This means that the enemy seeks to kill a man one question at a time.

Our minds have three recognized dimensions: conscious, subconscious, and the unconscious mind. The conscious mind represents what we are presently aware of. For example, if someone is standing in front of you, you are aware of their presence, or if someone is speaking to you, you are aware of their words. The subconscious mind represents things that affect us that we are unaware of. This part of our minds store memories, trauma, beliefs and habits. It is designed to protect us by housing beliefs, rejecting beliefs, and by determining how we react or respond to things present (people) and not present (plans). The unconscious mind consists of what our minds perform automatically. For example, our breathing is controlled by our unconscious mind. This is also the part of the mind that controls instinctual responses and houses forgotten trauma. The conscious mind's function is to help us survive.

Each level of our minds has a hierarchy, with the unconscious mind being at the top of that hierarchy and the conscious mind being the entrance or gateway. The enemy has to first access our conscious minds through the music we listen to, the people we affiliate ourselves with, the media we watch on television and the people we consider to be influential in our lives (celebrities, family members, leaders). For example, let's say that you meet a woman after church service is over and she asks you if you've seen the pastor. You are only consciously aware of her while she's standing in front of you, but you may not remember her because she has not played an important role in your life. However, if you were to meet that same woman after service and she were to begin prophesying to you, she is not only accessing your conscious world, but she's accessing the outer courts of your subconscious world using the power of words. Of course, if the prophecy comes from God and He confirms it, you will likely "believe it in" mean-

111

ing, you will let it into the second level of your subconscious mind ... the part of you that's in charge of making decisions. If you don't believe it, it will not go past your conscious mind, or it may go to the outer courts of your subconscious where it'll be challenged, questioned and possibly even cast down if it is found to be untrue.

The unconscious portion (inner courts) of the mind is at the top of the hierarchy. It's the part of you that affects you without your permission. This is the part of the mind that the enemy tries to get the closest to (because he cannot enter), but to do this, he must first find a way to enter you through your conscious. Thankfully, once we get saved, demons cannot enter our spirit because that's where the Holy Spirit lives. It is the Holy of Holies from within us, and demons cannot enter or possess this portion of us. The unconscious mind controls our breathing. It is where the breath of God circulates from within us. The word "breath" is synonymous with "spirit." This part of the believer is off-limits to Satan. For this reason, the kingdom of darkness will try to advance within a person in an attempt to get closest to the unconscious mind or third level of the soul. So, if you're listening to ungodly music, the enemy can start to change your beliefs and desensitize you to sin through that music, or if you're hanging around ungodly family members, he can use them to *sear* or *dry out* whatever level of your mind they have access to. After he's successfully entered the conscious mind, he will work to enter the subconscious mind by using the people in your life to cause you to establish beliefs, habits, fears and desires. This portion of your mind also controls your emotions. **1 Corinthians 15:33 (ESV):** *Be not deceived: evil communications corrupt good manners.*

The subconscious mind has three levels, with each level representing an advancement towards the unconscious mind. The first level is the introductory part of the mind. This is where new information that is being considered is housed. This means that you have not believed the information enough to let it into the second level of your belief system. However, you have not necessarily rejected the information either, so it sits in the first level of the subconscious where it is reviewed, tested and considered. For example, if someone tells you that your favorite celebrity is dead, but you don't necessarily trust the individual who brought the news to you, you will house the information in the outer courts of your subconscious mind. This means that even when the messenger (person who brought you the news) is no longer in your presence (conscious), you will retain what he or she told you in the outer courts of your subconscious. This puts the information on the forefront of your mind, close to the conscious where it can be easily cast out. To

113

move it in or out, you will likely call a friend or conduct an internet search to see if the information is factual. If it is, you will receive it as a fact and it'll enter the second level of your subconscious. If it isn't true, you'll reject it and cast it out of your mind.

Note: What we receive as a fact is what we understand in the natural sense, but what we receive as truth is what we receive as supernatural. For example, if someone dies, in the natural, it is a fact that they have ceased to live in the realm of the earth, but spiritually speaking, we know that they are still alive. They are in the presence of God. Their bodies have ceased to lived but not their spirit. Facts don't require faith; they only require evidence, but truth can only be received by faith.

The second level is where most demonic spirits lodge themselves. This is the level where we house most of the information that we have learned in school, from friends, etc. This is the level that we store information we consider to be "facts" but not necessarily "truth." What's the difference? Facts are conclusions drawn up by man and substantiated by some form of physical evidence. The Word of God is "Truth," however, what we receive as truth for our own lives is what we've received into the third or highest points of our subconscious mind.

We store faith and many of our religious beliefs in the third level of our subconscious. This is the level that we guard the most. Whatever we allow into this level is what's most important to us; it's what sits above our understanding. This is the information that many of us will defend with our lives; it is the information that's no longer up for questioning. It is truth to us. Therefore, it is one with us. Whatever we receive as truth is what becomes us. The world runs off facts, but believers live by the truth.

When a person allows facts to dwell in the third level of their subconscious, that person has no choice but to place truth in the second level. This means that the truth (supernatural information) is now being filtered by facts (natural information). Such a man is leaning to his own understanding and when this happens, he will become legalistic, religious, double-minded and unstable. Such a person is not grounded and has no anchor. **Hebrews 6:16-20 (ESV):** *For people swear by something greater than themselves, and in all their disputes an oath is final for confirmation. So when God desired to show more convincingly to the heirs of the promise the unchangeable character of his purpose, he guaranteed it with an oath, so that by two unchangeable things, in which it is impossible for God to lie, we who have fled for refuge might have strong encouragement to hold fast to* *the hope set before us. We have this as a sure and stead-fast anchor of the soul, a hope that enters into the inner place behind the curtain, where Jesus has gone as a fore-runner on our behalf, having become a high priest forever after the order of Melchizedek.*

If a man continues to fill himself with facts, he will eventually reject the truth and become agnostic or atheist, meaning, he has now exchanged the truth of God for a lie. This is the reason that demons are determined to advance from the first and second levels of the outer court and make their way to the outskirts of the inner court (the level of truth). Again, they cannot enter the unconscious mind or inner court, but they will advance towards it. The closest they got to the inner court, the most damage they can do to that person and through that person.

Ephesians 4:11-16 (ESV): *And he gave the apostles, the prophets, the evangelists, the shepherds and teachers, to equip the saints for the work of ministry, for building up the body of Christ, until we all attain to the unity of the faith and of the knowledge of the Son of God, to mature manhood, to the measure of the stature of the fullness of Christ, so that we may no longer be children, tossed to and fro by the waves and carried about by every wind of doctrine, by human cunning, by craftiness in deceitful schemes. Rather, speaking the truth in love, we are to* *grow up in every way into him who is the head, into Christ, from whom the whole body, joined and held together by every joint with which it is equipped, when each part is working properly, makes the body grow so that it builds itself up in love.*

Hebrews 6:16-20 (ESV): *For people swear by something greater than themselves, and in all their disputes an oath is final for confirmation. So when God desired to show more convincingly to the heirs of the promise the unchangeable character of his purpose, he guaranteed it with an oath, so that by two unchangeable things, in which it is impossible for God to lie, we who have fled for refuge might have strong encouragement to hold fast to the hope set before us. We have this as a sure and steadfast anchor of the soul, a hope that enters into the inner place behind the curtain, where Jesus has gone as a forerunner on our behalf, having become a high priest forever after the order of Melchizedek.*

Romans 1:24-25 (ESV): *Therefore God gave them up in the lusts of their hearts to impurity, to the dishonoring of their bodies among themselves, because they exchanged the truth about God for a lie and worshiped and served the creature rather than the Creator, who is blessed forever! Amen.*

Many believers have stored the truth in the same arena of their hearts as they've stored facts and this is why many believers are unstable. Their facts are always contending with the truth and they don't know which set of information to believe. When truth does not dwell in the third level of the subconscious, that level will be overrun by demons. This is when we start witnessing people demonstrate psychotic behavior and extreme instability. Once this level has been breached, the man is now in danger of receiving a reprobate mind if he does not repent.

1 Corinthians 3:16 (ESV): *Do you not know that you are God's temple and that God's Spirit dwells in you?*

Genesis 2:7 (ESV): *And the LORD God formed man of the dust of the ground, and breathed into his nostrils the breath of life; and man became a living soul.*

When a demonic spirit enters the third level of the subconscious, it has entered the level that's closest to the inner courts of a man (unconscious mind). From there, it can move more freely and can cause infirmities or establish new laws in that man's life. For example, it can tell the man that he cannot walk on his own. When a demonic spirit enters the third level of a man's subconscious mind, that man will likely have to go through several deliverances to get set free. The deliverance minister has to first cast out the demons in the first two layers of the subconscious in order to make his way to the outskirts of the inner court. The first two layers of the subconscious are broad so the deliverance minister can't just advance into the third level; he must first move horizontally through the outer courts into each chamber of the infected man's heart. This means that he has to cast out the demons that are affecting that man's beliefs and habits. After this, the partially delivered man must receive counseling to maintain his deliverance, which means that he'll need to establish new, godly beliefs. He'll have to allow the truth he knows to rise above the facts he's received. When this happens, the deliverance minister can now see what's hiding in the third level because the outer courts are now filled with the light of God and darkness can no longer dwell there. That light will then radiate into the third level, thus, allowing the deliverance minister to see what's lurking in the dark places with the help of the Holy Spirit. Once the third level of the outer courts has been cleaned out, the light of God and the love of God can now dwell in that man and if he was unable to walk, he will suddenly stand to his feet and perform what was once impossible for him. That's because the *fact* that he could not walk is then overridden by the *truth* that he is healed through the blood of Jesus Christ.

Isaiah 53:4-5 (ESV): *Surely he has borne our griefs and carried our sorrows; yet we esteemed him stricken, smitten by God, and afflicted. But he was pierced for our transgressions; he was crushed for our iniquities; upon* *him was the chastisement that brought us peace, and with his wounds we are healed.*

CHAPTER 6

Stalked by Jezebel

1 **Kings 18:17-46 (ESV):** *When Ahab saw Elijah, Ahab said to him, "Is it you, you troubler of Israel?" And he answered, "I have not troubled Israel, but you have, and your father's house, because you have abandoned the commandments of the Lord and followed the Baals. Now therefore send and gather all Israel to me at Mount Carmel, and the 450 prophets of Baal and the 400 prophets of Asherah, who eat at Jezebel's table."*

So Ahab sent to all the people of Israel and gathered the prophets together at Mount Carmel. And Elijah came near to all the people and said, "How long will you go limping between two different opinions? If the Lord is God, follow him; but if Baal, then follow him." And the people did not answer him a word. Then Elijah said to the people, "I, even I only, am left a prophet of the Lord, but Baal's prophets are 450 men. Let two bulls be given to us, and let them choose one bull for themselves and cut it in pieces and lay it on the wood, but put no fire to it. And I will prepare the other bull and lay it on the wood and put no fire to it. And you call upon the name of your god, and

I will call upon the name of the Lord, and the God who an-swers by fire, he is God." And all the people answered, "It is well spoken." Then Elijah said to the prophets of Baal, "Choose for yourselves one bull and prepare it first, for you are many, and call upon the name of your god, but put no fire to it." And they took the bull that was given them, and they prepared it and called upon the name of Baal from morning until noon, saying, "O Baal, answer us!" But there was no voice, and no one answered. And they limped around the altar that they had made. And at noon Elijah mocked them, saying, "Cry aloud, for he is a god. Either he is musing, or he is relieving himself, or he is on a journey, or perhaps he is asleep and must be awak-ened." And they cried aloud and cut themselves after their custom with swords and lances, until the blood gushed out upon them. And as midday passed, they raved on until the time of the offering of the oblation, but there was no voice. No one answered; no one paid attention.

Then Elijah said to all the people, "Come near to me." And all the people came near to him. And he repaired the altar of the Lord that had been thrown down. Elijah took twelve stones, according to the number of the tribes of the sons of Jacob, to whom the word of the Lord came, saying, "Israel shall be your name," and with the stones he built an altar in the name of the Lord. And he made a trench about the altar, as great as would contain two seahs of seed. And he put the wood in order and cut the bull in pieces and laid it on the wood. And he said, "Fill four jars with water and pour it on the burnt offering and on the wood." And he said, "Do it a second time." And they did it a second time. And he said, "Do it a third time." And they did it a third time. And the water ran around the altar and filled the trench also with water.

And at the time of the offering of the oblation, Elijah the prophet came near and said, "O Lord, God of Abraham, Isaac, and Israel, let it be known this day that you are God in Israel, and that I am your servant, and that I have done all these things at your word. Answer me, O Lord, answer me, that this people may know that you, O Lord, are God, and that you have turned their hearts back." Then the fire of the Lord fell and consumed the burnt offering and the wood and the stones and the dust, and licked up the water that was in the trench. And when all the people saw it, they fell on their faces and said, "The Lord, he is God; the Lord, he is God." And Elijah said to them, "Seize the prophets of Baal; let not one of them escape." And they seized them. And Elijah brought them down to the brook Kishon and slaughtered them there.

And Elijah said to Ahab, "Go up, eat and drink, for there is a sound of the rushing of rain." So Ahab went up to eat and to drink. And Elijah went up to the top of Mount Carmel. And he bowed himself down on the earth and put his face between his knees. And he said to his servant, "Go up now, look toward the sea." And he went up and looked

and said, "There is nothing." And he said, "Go again," seven times. And at the seventh time he said, "Behold, a little cloud like a man's hand is rising from the sea." And he said, "Go up, say to Ahab, 'Prepare your chariot and go down, lest the rain stop you.'" And in a little while the heavens grew black with clouds and wind, and there was a great rain. And Ahab rode and went to Jezreel. And the hand of the Lord was on Elijah, and he gathered up his garment and ran before Ahab to the entrance of Jezreel.
1 Kings 19:1-3 (ESV): *Ahab told Jezebel all that Elijah had done, and how he had killed all the prophets with the sword. Then Jezebel sent a messenger to Elijah, saying, "So may the gods do to me and more also, if I do not make your life as the life of one of them by this time tomorrow." Then he was afraid, and he arose and ran for his life and came to Beersheba, which belongs to Judah, and left his servant there.*

Elijah was bold enough to confront Ahab. He was truly a soldier of God. He stood before a nation of people whose hearts had been turned away from God and he declared that JEHOVAH is God. He knew that he was standing before blood-thirsty pagans who'd likely assisted Jezebel in killing off so many of God's prophets, nevertheless, he obeyed God and God surely proved Himself to be God. What a great victory that was! Jezebel's prophets were killed and the people of God turned their hearts back to the Lord. This was surely a Kingdom victory. Nevertheless, after the showdown was over and everyone had gone home, Elijah received a threatening message from Jezebel. Fearing for his life, Elijah went on the run.

I believe everyone who has ever read this story questioned Elijah's fear. How could the same bold prophet who'd just witnessed God rain fire down from Heaven turn around and run from a mere woman? The truth of the matter is ... even though Elijah was anointed by God, he was still human.

Have you ever been teaching or preaching and you felt the anointing on you strongly? At that moment, you felt invincible; you knew that God's angels were standing around you with their swords drawn. You knew that the enemy couldn't touch you if he wanted to. Nevertheless, once the shouting and the sweating was over, you didn't feel so immortal anymore. You pretty much shrunk back into being a mere man or woman. That's what happened with Elijah. He felt the power of God on him strongly when he'd confronted Ahab and the prophets of Baal, but when Jezebel sent a threat to him, he allowed fear to chase away his faith. Fear turned to terror and Elijah went on the run. Elijah could have easily confronted and taken down Jezebel, but in a moment's time, he'd allowed fear in. Many of God's prophets are guilty of doing the same.

It was the year 2008 and I was but a young woman in Christ. I wasn't new to Christianity, but I was still somewhat young in the faith. Nevertheless, God had placed a bold word in my mouth and I wasn't ashamed to share it with anyone who wanted to hear.

I had just gotten remarried and my then-husband was living in Germany while I was still in the United States. After having been rebuked by the Lord, I had just shut down a hip hop website I was running and I committed to working only for the Kingdom of God. My trade was web design, so I started designing websites for ministries and I loved what I did. Nevertheless, my fees were *very* low and, of course, this brought me the wrong types of customers. I didn't think too much about my fees at that time because I was excited about being able to work with Christian leaders. I'd spoken and worked with a few leaders and I loved the wisdom that had been shared with me. At that time, I didn't know what a Jezebel spirit was, even though I'd vaguely heard of the infamous Jezebel in the Bible.

One day, I received an email from a woman who said she wanted to hire me to design her website (we'll call her Nancy). Nancy said she was a pastor and an author, and for me, both of those titles were *big*. I'd only been saved for eight or nine years and I had an enormous amount of love and respect for my own pastor, so I pretty much had that same amount of love and respect for other pastors. Additionally, I was a small town woman who'd never met an author before, so it goes without saying, I was all too eager to work with Nancy.

I emailed my number to Nancy after we discussed pricing and a few details over the internet. When Nancy called me, I pretty much acted like a star-struck teenager who'd just received a call from her favorite pop star. Nevertheless, I had never heard of Nancy; she wasn't a well-known pastor. As a matter of fact, time revealed that Nancy didn't even have a church. Howbeit, I wasn't impressed with her name; it was the title itself that I reverenced.

My conversation with Nancy went really well. She asked me a lot of questions about myself and she told me a lot of things about herself. *Nowadays, this behavior is a red flag to me because time has taught me that customers who do this are attempting to establish a soul tie.* Anyhow, Nancy asked me a few questions about my pricing, my timeline to completion and to see a portfolio of my work. I answered her questions and sent her a link to my portfolio. After that, she asked me to send her an invoice so she could pay me the deposit I required and I did. But that wasn't enough. Nancy began to share with me some of the things she'd gone through with her estranged husband. I'd learned a lot with my previous divorce and even though I was still somewhat of a babe in Christ, I could not deny the Word of God that was within me. I found myself encouraging Nancy and testifying about my experiences with my ex-husband. I told her how the Lord had protected me, healed me, and instructed me throughout my marriage and my divorce. Nancy listened intently, only stopping to tell me how anointed I was and how she believed I was called to evangelism. *I smiled.* I knew I had a heart for God, but Nancy was the first person to give me a label, so it goes without saying that I fancied talking with her ... *in the beginning.*

Nancy started calling me every day and at first, this didn't alarm me because I was working on her website. We'd discuss the details about her site and then, she'd start talking about her marital problems and life's problems all over again. I was young in the faith, so I was elated at the opportunity to encourage a woman I believed to be a pastor. Truthfully, I felt honored and I wanted to prove to God that He could trust me. I'd spent most of my life trying to prove myself and my loyalty to the wrong people and I felt like I had been granted a unique opportunity to prove my loyalty to God by being loyal to His people. One brother-in-Christ that I'd met had been telling me that I was anointed and God was going to use me to do big things, so I thought Nancy was my first test. I didn't want to fail it; I couldn't fail it.

In less than a week, I'd finished Nancy's website and I'd began to notice some things about Nancy that made me uneasy. First, she kept changing her mind about the site's arrangement, the site's content, and so on. I could tell that she was trying to hold on to me, but giving me more work to do was a cruel way to do it. Nevertheless, I would finish Nancy's requests in a matter of minutes or hours and I'd send her an email declaring the site was finished all over again. That's when I'd get another email from Nancy requesting more work, more changes, and more of my time. I would also get inundated with phone calls and each call would last two or more hours. I felt bullied and I felt like my time and my business were both being taken over by Nancy. She wanted me to work exclusively for her and she'd get noticeably jealous anytime I said I was working on another client's project. But Nancy was a pastor. How could I set her straight? *You can't yell at a pastor,* I thought to myself. I would just have to find another way to let Nancy know that I couldn't dedicate my every waking moment to either working for her or talking with her. It goes without saying that she wasn't giving me any extra money either. She was simply taking over and I felt it.

One day, Nancy called me and said the Lord had spoken to her regarding me. She said that He told her I was an evangelist and that she was to be my pastor. I already had a pastor, but at the same time, Nancy was acknowledging the fact that I had a call on my life. It was a hard decision to make, so I told Nancy I would pray about it. It didn't matter to Nancy though. She drafted up a certificate of ordination, asked me for my mailing address and mailed the certificate to me. She also told me to place my name on her website as one of "her" evangelists. Even though I was young in the faith, I found myself cringing every time she referred to me as "my evangelist." Her tone, mannerisms, and controlling ways made me uneasy. Before long, I began to question whether God had sent Nancy to me. I also began to pray about Nancy and it didn't take long for God to answer my prayers.

I'd met a new friend while out walking one day (I think I met her a little before I met Nancy). Clara lived in my neighborhood and I'd met her while walking my dog. Clara was my age and when I met her, I was walking on a narrow sidewalk on my normal walking route. I tried to move over as much as I could to let Clara pass me by, but instead of walking past me, she started walking with me. We talked about my dog, life and just about everything we could think of. I found out that like me, Clara walked every day and wanted a walking buddy, so we agreed to meet up every day before we walked. Clara was really nice and we had a lot in common. She wasn't controlling; she was just normal. She was a single woman and my husband lived in Germany, so I had a lot of time on my hands. Honestly, we were both obsessed with the idea of being married. I'd just gotten remarried and Clara wanted to get married someday. Clara and I became close friends almost instantly and we utilized every opportunity we had to talk about men.

One day, Clara and I were out walking and we started talking about funny movies we liked to watch. Suddenly, my phone started ringing. It was Nancy and I knew that she wasn't going to want to get off the phone, so I ignored her call. Clara noticed a change in me after the call, so I explained my situation to her. Being a babe in Christ herself, Clara couldn't offer me too much advice, but she did tell me to "go off" on Nancy. That did seem like the easy way out, but there had to be another way. I laughed, but I thought that if I yelled at Nancy, I'd be struck by lightning or something to that effect. That's when my phone started ringing again. I remembered a few times when I didn't answer Nancy's calls. She would always hang up and call me again and again until I answered. Then, she would proceed to question why I hadn't answered my phone. I didn't want to be inundated with phone calls, so I decided to answer my phone and tell her that I'd call her back. "What are you doing? I just called you," said Nancy. I explained to her that I was out walking with my friend Clara and I told her I'd call her back. "When? What time?" asked Nancy. "I don't know," I said. "Maybe in an hour or two. I'm out walking with Clara." Nancy paused and there was a silence on the line that seemed to go on forever. "Hello?" My agitation could be heard in my voice. *"Helloooooo?"* Nancy finally let out a sigh. "I'll give you *one* hour. That's *one* hour because we've got work to do," she said grudgingly before hanging up the phone. Clara pretty much heard most of what Nancy said. She waited until she was sure that I was off the phone before speaking. "Is she funny?" asked Clara jokingly. *(Funny is a term often used by southerners and it means gay.)* "I don't know," I laughed. "She sure acts like it."

True to her word, Nancy called me back in an hour. She didn't ask me where I was, if Clara was still with me or if I felt like talking ... *nothing.* She just started talking and I had to interrupt her. "Nancy, I have to call you back. Clara and I are about to watch a movie." I could feel the tension on the line. Honestly, it was strange to see a woman behaving like that towards another woman. In my heart, I was beginning to question Nancy's sexuality, but how could she be gay? She's a pastor! I didn't realize that I was in the trenches of a Jezebel spirit and she had already started weaving me into her web of deception. Again, at that time, I had never heard of the Jezebel spirit.

"I'll hold," said Nancy. Obviously, she didn't hear me. I'd just told her that I was about to watch a movie and I'd call her back. Movies generally last two hours and there was no way that I was about to lay my phone down for two hours while Nancy sat on the other line and listened in. "No," I said. "I'm about to watch a movie. I'll call you back." Nancy wasted no time responding. "I'll hold," she said in a stern voice. I stood to my feet. I couldn't believe what I was hearing. "Nancy, I'll call you back," I said firmly. "I'm about to watch a movie with Clara." The line was silent and then, Nancy said it again. "I'll give you *one* hour because we've got work to do!" She then hung up the line and I sat down and tried to understand what was going on.

I started looking for ways to get rid of Nancy. I was finished with her website and I knew I did not want her to be my pastor. I started becoming more and more agitated with her. She would call me from the moment I got off work and she'd keep calling me throughout the day. One day, she'd called and asked me in the most wicked tone, "Am I controlling?" Finally! She was starting to see the error of her ways ... *or so I thought.* Maybe she'd had an epiphany; maybe the Lord had dealt with her. After all, I was praying for strategies to get away from her. "Yes," I said, thinking that she'd apologize and try to be a better person. Nancy's response only escalated my disgust towards her. She laughed. "Yeah, I know," she said in the most wicked tone. The only apologetic-sounding thing she said was that she doesn't try to be controlling, but she continued to laugh at the fact that she was controlling as if it were a good character trait to have. That's when I realized that Nancy liked being the way that she was. She was amused with her own behavior. I couldn't take much more of her, so I got off the phone with her.

I started realizing that something was seriously wrong with Nancy. She was about fifteen years older than me, but that did not justify her behaviors. My own pastor didn't act like that, so why was it okay for her to behave in such a manner? Our final two conversations left no room for doubt. I had to get away from Nancy and the only way I was going to do so was ... I had to *stop tolerating* her and just be rude. I had to take authority of the situation, otherwise, I was going to become nothing but a piece of Nancy's broken property.

One day, Nancy called me and asked, "Did your husband ever get that situation straight with his VISA? Will he be able to come to the U.S. or will you be moving to Germany?" At first, I didn't think too much about Nancy's question because obviously, I'd discussed the situation with her. "I don't know," I said. "I'm thinking I'll likely have to move to Germany, but I'm okay with that. I like Germany." Nancy got quiet and that's when she confirmed to me more than ever that God had not sent her. "I'll pray for him to come to the States," she said. "If he can't come here, I'll pay for your divorce." I was taken aback, astonished, shocked ... you name it, I felt it. I couldn't believe she'd just told me that she would pay for my divorce if my husband couldn't clear his VISA to the United States. "I'll call you back," I said, still holding on to the belief that I wasn't supposed to "go off" on a pastor. I then called my brother-in-Christ (Tony) and told him what happened. I was sincerely confused, but I knew that I wanted absolutely nothing to do with Nancy. I'd always despised controlling people and Nancy was more than controlling; she was a religious dictator.

Tony confirmed what I believed. He told me that she was trying to control me, God hadn't sent her and then, he told me to research the Jezebel spirit. "That's a Jezebel spirit," Tony said. "Who the heck is Jezebel?" I asked. Tony told me to research the Jezebel spirit so I could better understand what I was dealing with. I didn't take Tony's advice immediately because I was actively looking for a quick way to get away from Nancy that would not result in me getting struck by lightning. Again, I was young in the faith; I didn't know any better.

A day or two later, I got another call from Nancy. I didn't answer my phone because I didn't want to talk with her. Nevertheless, true to her character, she kept calling my phone until I answered. When I answered the phone, Nancy was on the other end shouting in excitement. Her ministry (ironically enough) was geared towards hurting women and according to Nancy, she'd just gotten a contractual offer from some corporation who wanted to sponsor her ministry. "Pack your bags!" shouted Nancy excitedly. "We're about to travel the world!" I couldn't get excited. I wanted *nothing* to do with Nancy. I had never physically met her, but she'd already became the ugliest person I knew. I congratulated her on her new sponsor, but then, I told her that I wouldn't be able to travel with her. Of course, she wanted to know why. "You know, I just got married," I said. "My husband and I are newlyweds and he wants to have children." There was a long (cold) silence on the line. "Children?" Nancy asked scoffingly. "Yes, children," I said confidently. Nancy countered by asking me the same question in a sterner tone maybe three or four times. "Children?!" Nevertheless, I answered her each time with more confidence in my voice. "Yes, children; we want children," I said. Finally, Nancy's venom shot out of her mouth. "I'll pray for you to have *one* child; you hear me? *One!* Because we've got work to do! Anyhow, one of my girlfriends used to be married to an African man and all he wanted to do was keep her barefoot and pregnant. She had to divorce his behind!" I couldn't take it anymore. I got off the phone with Nancy and my mind was made up. I could not and would not talk with her anymore. How dare she tell me how many children she was going to pray for me to have as if she had dominion over my love life and my womb? She was definitely not a God-send and I knew I couldn't talk with her anymore without being disrespectful. I knew that I was gonna finally "go off" if I spoke with her again and I'd be repenting at the first sound of thunder.

Later that day, I received a call from a friend of mine named "Serenity." Serenity was not a babe in Christ and I knew I could confide in her. I told her about my run-ins with Nancy and all of the things she'd said and did to me. "Oh, no sis. That's Jezebel," said Serenity. Finally, that name got my attention. "Jezebel?" I questioned. I had to sit down. Brother Tony was obviously on to something. "Who's Jezebel?" I asked inquisitively. "It's a demonic spirit that likes to control people." Serenity went on to tell me about a pastor she'd once had ... a woman she said was definitely under the influence of the Jezebel spirit. I asked a lot of questions and with that, Serenity told me to do some research online. When I did, I came across a video on YouTube that described the Jezebel spirit. The video was 40 minutes long and it made the hair on the back of my neck stand up. I felt like the commentator personally knew Nancy and had created that video about her. He described Nancy's personality thoroughly, leaving nothing uncovered. Being young in Christ, I started getting scared. A demon? I had been talking on the phone with an *actual* demon? I knew that there was *no way* I was going to talk with Nancy again.

Getting away from Nancy was not as easy as I thought it would be. I tried to take the passive way out and just stop answering her phone calls. I was done with her site and I'd already sent her all of her passwords; there was nothing else that she needed from me. But Nancy saw things differently. She called repeatedly and before long, she started leaving me very condescending messages. She also inundated me with emails accusing me of being demon-possessed and telling me to stop listening to the devil. Of course, I didn't tell her about any of my conversations; I'd just stopped answering her calls. One day, I decided to answer the call and simply tell her to stop calling me, but before I could get a word out, Nancy let out a long sigh and said, "Let me speak with your mother." Her tone couldn't have sounded any more wicked. I hung up the phone. A few minutes later, she called me again. "Just stop calling me!" I yelled after I answered the line. That's when Nancy started yelling, "I'm coming to your state! I'm coming to your city! You don't know who you've been messing with! I'm gonna expose you to your pastor!" I got tired of hearing her, so I hung up the line. I couldn't get her last sentence out of my mind. *Expose? Expose what?* The only thing I'd ever talked with her about was God and I'd never even said a negative word about my husband. There was *nothing* to expose. Nevertheless, I suddenly remembered something the commentator said in the video that I'd watched. He said that Jezebels are always threatening to expose the people they cannot control.

Nancy kept emailing me about the certificate of ordination she'd sent me. "I better not hear that you've been using that certificate to do ministry or I'll sue you for everything you've got!" she wrote. I didn't respond. I just blocked her email. That was the third or fourth email address she'd created to write me from because I kept blocking her emails. When she called me, I knew she was calling about the certificate. I didn't want that certificate. I wanted nothing to do with Nancy or her ministry. I didn't want to be "her" evangelist. "You better send me that certificate back in the mail and I better not hear about you using it!" she screamed. I was calm. Honestly, I just wanted it all to be over with. I wanted Nancy to leave me alone once and for all. "Nancy, I'm putting it in the mail first thing in the morning. Now please, leave me alone," I said before hanging up the line. True to my word, I sent the certificate back to her. Amazingly enough, I had never really pulled the certificate out of the envelope she'd sent me. I didn't have peace with it, so I'd opened the envelope, peered in it and placed it on the television set. It sat there until I sent it back to Nancy. I didn't take any chances. I sent it back priority mail with tracking. I didn't want her to say that she hadn't received it because it was clear to me that she did not want to turn me loose.

The last call I got from Nancy was nothing short of a direct threat. I answered the phone ready to tell her that I was going to file stalking charges against her, but I didn't get a chance to say a word. "You better watch your back!" screamed Nancy in the angriest, most hateful tone I'd ever heard. She didn't wait for me to respond. She simply hung up and somehow, I knew that was the last call I would ever receive from her. Over the years, I've received several friend requests from Nancy on Facebook and each time, she's used different names. On a couple of occasions, I accepted her as a friend on Facebook, but the Lord would always deal with me and I'd go back to my email, look for the email addresses that Nancy contacted me from and I'd search for them on Facebook. Amazingly enough, I found her no less than three times on my friend's list under different names. Of course, I deleted and blocked each one of her profiles (and personalities). This was a case of Jezebel stalking one of God's prophets.

I didn't realize the trauma I'd endured until another woman brought it up to me years later. I refused to go to church; I preferred to read the Word from the comforts and safety of my own home. I had come in contact with the Jezebel spirit a few times after Nancy, and I grew tired of fighting with it. Why was it after me? What did it want from me? *I'm not special*, I thought to myself. I was on the phone talking with "Apostle Marcia" one day and I began to share my testimony with her regarding Nancy. I'd opened up to her and started telling her a lot of things I'd gone through, but I wasn't using it to justify not going to church. Truthfully, I believed that God had me at home for a while (I still don't doubt that) and she'd confirmed it, but according to Apostle Marcia, that season had lifted. "Oh my God," said Apostle Marcia. "You're Elijah. I've been praying and asking God about you and trying to figure you out, but the Lord just revealed to me that you're like Elijah. You're hiding from Jezebel and your apartment is your cave." That revelation hit me pretty hard and I felt a strong confirmation in my spirit. I could feel the tears welling up in my eyes and the knot beginning to form in my belly. I was hiding from Jezebel. I'd been traumatized and I was so afraid that I'd join a Jezebel-led ministry that I opted to stay at home, even when God released me to come out of my cave. I'd moved to a different state by then, so I wasn't near my home church. I didn't trust most leaders and I wanted nothing to do with church or church folks. I just wanted God to be pleased with me. I wanted a solo ministry where I preached to and encouraged myself. By this time, I was no longer scared to "go off" on a leader, but I still had respect for leaders and leadership (I still do). I was no longer afraid of Jezebel either. I despised that spirit. I realized that I was afraid of getting caught up and finding myself becoming a part of a Jezebel ministry. I feared that I'd unintentionally sow into Jezebel's witchcraft and I'd endure years of hurt, pain, droughts, etc. as a result. By that time, I had studied the Jezebel spirit thoroughly and I could pretty much identify it in many of the women who had it. Nevertheless, my lesson was far from over. You see, there was much more to Jezebel than what I'd encountered and I needed to understand the Jezebel spirit if I was gonna ever be able to effectively war against it.

God was preparing me for the assignment He'd given

me. He allowed me to meet Nancy so that I could first hear the term "Jezebel spirit." Meeting Nancy provoked me to start researching and learning more about that spirit.

So why was the Jezebel spirit stalking me? Why does it stalk you? At first, when I asked myself that question, I thought there was something *special* about me that attracted that spirit. After a while, I started wondering if I had that spirit because it was so drawn to me, plus, I often taught that we attract what we are. Howbeit, God began to minister to me and something Apostle Marcia said to me helped me to get "over" myself to see the bigger picture. She said to me, "Tiffany, you are a prophet. Jezebel is going to *always* come after you." That was a powerful revelation and it helped me to stop thinking that there was something about me that attracted that spirit. Jezebel hates the prophets of God and will always pursue them. What I had to learn to do was take authority over every Jezebel spirit that came after me ... meaning, I don't just sit around and let Jezebel take my time, energy, peace or whatever it is that demon is trying to steal from me.

Another reason the Jezebel spirit stalks people is because it is attracted to power and authority. God has given mankind dominion over the Earth and everything in it; He has given the believer dominion over all the works of the enemy. We have the power of God operating in us and we have the ability to walk in the authority of God. Satan comes to steal, kill and destroy; we know this, but we must understand that there are different types of demonic spirits and each one works to steal, kill or destroy something specifically from us. For example, a lust spirit comes to pervert the people of God and keep us from walking in holiness. It comes to bind us with ungodly soul ties and it wants to use us to bind others with ungodly soul ties. The spirits of suicide, premature death and murder come to steal lives. The spirit of infirmity comes to steal our wholeness, health and well-being. It also comes to take away our abilities to function in the natural as well as the spirit. The spirit of doubt and unbelief comes to steal our peace and our faith. All the same, the Jezebel spirit comes to steal our power, dominion and authority.

The Jezebel spirit is attracted to fear and Ahab is synonymous with fear. Anytime a believer (or unbeliever) does not walk in the authority that God has given him or her, Jezebel will pursue that person. Why is that? Jezebel sees power and it also sees a person who is afraid to tap into that power. Each person has the ability to cause something to move in the realm of the Earth. Of course, each person's faith determines what it is that that particular person has the ability to move. For example, even though a mustard seed is tiny, not every believer has faith the size of a mustard seed.

Matthew 17:20 (ESV): *He said to them, "Because of your little faith. For truly, I say to you, if you have faith like a grain of mustard seed, you will say to this mountain, 'Move from here to there,' and it will move, and nothing will be impossible for you."*

When Jesus described the measure of faith we ought to have, He was telling us that every measure of faith has the ability to move something of a certain size. He used a mustard seed, which is one of the smallest seeds in the Earth and contrasted it with a mountain, which is one of the largest piles of dirt on Earth. In short, He was telling us to build upon our faith by planting a seed of faith so that it can grow. Jezebel sees the power within us and it also sees that we are too afraid to tap into that power, so whenever it sees a person (believer or unbeliever) who is not utilizing their own power and authority, it will pursue them. For example, I was afraid to offend Nancy because of my lack of understanding. Sure, we need to respect our leaders, but we first need to test the spirit behind every leader we decide to follow. Respecting a person or an office does not mean that we allow that person or anyone working in a specific office to tread upon us. The Bible tells us that we will know them by their fruit (Matthew 7:16). If I knew enough of the Word back then, I would have known that I didn't have to take what I took from Nancy. I was supposed to guard my heart (Proverbs 4:23) by testing the spirits (1 John 4:1), taking authority over all the works of darkness (Luke 10:19) and fearing God, not man (Matthew 10:28, Proverbs 29:25, Psalm 118:6). Additionally, I was not supposed to tolerate Jezebel (Revelation 2:20).

Jezebel is attracted to timidity; that spirit will always pursue a person who walks in any level of fear, whether you refer to that fear as outright fear, timidity or shyness. That's because again, the believer has a level of authority that he or she is not walking in and Jezebel will happily walk in that authority for them ... only it will use their power and authority against them and against the Kingdom of God. So, if Tina, for example, is a shy believer, Tina is going to attract Jezebel to herself. The enemy will likely send people to hurt Tina because by not walking in the authority that God has given her, Tina is unguarded. She's also in rebellion, which the Bible tells us is the same as the sin of witchcraft (1 Samuel 15:23). For this reason, the enemy can and will send people after her. *Understand this: witches are attracted to witchcraft, so when a person enters rebellion, they draw witches to themselves.* Because of her rebellion, Tina may find herself being hurt by men, harassed by women and tormented by spirits. After tormenting her, Satan will send a dominant Jezebel-infested soul into her life. Let's say that person's name is Lola. Lola will encourage Tina, console her when she's hurt and come against her enemies for her. In Lola's hurt, anger and bitterness, she will see Tina as her own personal opportunity to redeem herself. She's not protecting Tina because she loves her; she's just doing what she knows how to do and that is to fight. When she came across Tina, Tina presented her an opportunity to fight on her behalf and she couldn't resist taking it. What you are witnessing here is two broken souls who have become co-dependent on one another. By walking in fear and not utilizing the power, authority and dominion that God has given her, Tina has picked up an Ahab spirit. By trying to usurp the authority given to others, Lola has picked up the Jezebel spirit. Jezebels are attracted to Ahabs. At the same time, Lola will likely despise Tina, nevertheless, she will see the benefits of keeping her around. She can get Tina to run her errands and Tina makes Lola feel better about herself. The demon in Lola needs Tina's power and authority to do its evil deeds, so whenever Tina is hurting or frustrated, little does she know, she uses her ability to loose things in the realm of the Earth. She confides in Lola and pretty much gives Lola permission to walk in her authority against whomever it is that she feels has been affecting her in a negative way. By utilizing the power to bind and loose in an evil way, Lola and Tina are both guilty of witchcraft. Just as Ahab is synonymous with fear, Jezebel is synonymous with witchcraft.

It doesn't matter what you fear doing; wherever there is fear in your life, Jezebel will take up residence. Fear opposes faith and faith opposes fear. There is only one kind of fear that we are allowed to operate in and that is the fear of God.

Proverbs 1:7 (ESV): *The fear of the LORD is the beginning of knowledge; fools despise wisdom and instruction.*

1 Peter 2:17 (ESV): *Honor everyone. Love the brotherhood. Fear God. Honor the emperor.*

Ecclesiastes 5:7 (ESV): *For when dreams increase and words grow many, there is vanity; but God is the one you must fear.*

To fear God is synonymous with having faith in God. Anytime you fear something or someone, you are acknowledging that thing or that person's power ... whether that power be perceived or actual. God's power is actual; He is omnipotent (all-powerful), sovereign (possessing unlimited power) and almighty (possessing complete power). To fear Him is to acknowledge His power. The Bible goes on to tell us that perfect love casts out fear.

1 John 4:18 (ESV): *There is no fear in love, but perfect love casts out fear. For fear has to do with punishment, and whoever fears has not been perfected in love.*

What does this mean? When we come to Christ, we are kept by our fear of Him; we acknowledge His sovereignty, His power, and His might. Nevertheless, as we get to know Him, we are no longer kept by our fear of Him. It is our love for Him (made perfect) that keeps us. For example, a toddler doesn't necessarily understand love. If you have a one-year-old son, his love for you is not yet mature enough to be perfect. For this reason, he honors you because of his familiarity with you, his natural bond with you, and his fear of you. His love for you will remain imperfect for the majority of his childhood and young adulthood because he does not yet understand the fullness of love. As he matures, it is his love for you that will compel him to make the right decisions regarding you. That's why immature adults depend on their parents, but mature adults take care of their parents. When we come to know and love the Lord, we no longer choose to do what's right because of our fear of Him; it is our love for Him that compels us to do the right thing. Now, if our love is not yet made perfect, we will default to and be kept by our fear of Him. At the same time, age does not determine maturity. There are some forty and fifty-year-old men and women who solely and selfishly depend on their parents ... not because they "need" their parents, but because they are too lazy and immature to take care of themselves. Their love for their parents is not yet perfect, which means they are immature and self-centered.

When we fear God, we are led by the Word because of our fear, but when we love God, we are led by the Word in love. In other words, *mature* love casts out fear. Of course, we are imperfect creatures, but the Bible does not say imperfect *people* cast out fear; it's perfect *love* that casts out fear. How can an imperfect person give perfect love? God is love and He is perfect. When we, as imperfect people, love the Lord with all of our heart, soul and mind, we are operating in perfect love. This means we are holding nothing back from God because we are fully surrendered and submitted to Him. It also means that we know Him personally and intimately. You cannot love someone you do not know.

When we walk after the flesh, we are being led by our sinful, uncrucified nature. It is this very nature that draws the Jezebel spirit.
Galatians 5:16-24 (ESV): *But I say, walk by the Spirit, and you will not gratify the desires of the flesh. For the desires of the flesh are against the Spirit, and the desires of the Spirit are against the flesh, for these are opposed to*

each other, to keep you from doing the things you want to do. But if you are led by the Spirit, you are not under the law. Now the works of the flesh are evident: sexual immorality, impurity, sensuality, idolatry, sorcery, enmity, strife, jealousy, fits of anger, rivalries, dissensions, divisions, envy, drunkenness, orgies, and things like these. I warn you, as I warned you before, that those who do such things will not inherit the kingdom of God. But the fruit of the Spirit is love, joy, peace, patience, kindness, goodness, faithfulness, gentleness, self-control; against such things there is no law. And those who belong to Christ Jesus have crucified the flesh with its passions and desires.

When we do not walk in love, we will walk in fear and the Jezebel spirit smells, craves, and is drawn to fear. Fear doesn't always manifest through trembling and avoidance. Sometimes, we are drawn to the very things and people that we fear. For example, some men ally themselves with their enemies out of fear. This is the same thing that Ahab did. He allied himself with the very nation that he feared. Some Jezebels fear other higher-ranking Jezebels and because of this, they are drawn to them. A good example would be a co-worker of yours who buys gifts for the manager and is always going into the manager's office. Let's say that the manager has the infamous Jezebel spirit. Your co-worker is always telling the manager about any and everyone who does not follow the manager's directions. Even though the manager did not promote her, summon her or give her the authority to reprimand anyone, she feels compelled to do the things that she does. There are a few reasons for her behavior. One of those reasons is ... she fears the manager. She believes that if she buys gifts for the manager and tells on everyone who does not perform their jobs correctly, she is securing her job and position. In other words, she is acknowledging the manager's power and ability to reprimand, demote, and terminate the people in that office, including herself. Secondly, she does this because of selfish ambition. She wants to be promoted and she believes that by doing the things that she does, the manager will see her as loyal, dedicated, and mature. She hopes that this will compel the manager to promote and favor her. Next, she does this in an attempt to usurp the manager's authority. Since she, herself, does not possess the power to reprimand, demote or terminate any of the employees, she tries to utilize the manager's ability to do so. This is her way of controlling the employees through the manager. This is in no doubt the Jezebel spirit.

If the manager has the Jezebel spirit, the co-worker in question will submit herself as a low-level Jezebel. This means that she is willing to double as an Ahab spirit where the manager is involved. In other words, she is willing to relinquish her authority to the manager whenever she wants to operate in and through it. If the manager does not have a Jezebel spirit, the co-worker will still acknowledge the manager's power and ability to promote, demote, reprimand and terminate herself and others. For this reason, she will try to win favor with the manager or she will try to get the manager terminated. Because she is infected with the Jezebel spirit, her main focus is gaining or usurping power.

Some people are stalked by the Jezebel spirit because they have power, authority and dominion that they are afraid to walk in. For this reason, such individuals will find themselves being stalked by people who have the Jezebel spirit. A good example would be a woman who keeps attracting and involving herself with abusive men. An abusive man has the Jezebel spirit ... there are no exceptions to this. They are physically, mentally, verbally and financially abusive because they don't possess the power to control others, so they use the abilities that they do have to manipulate and control others using the spirit of fear. In other words, they are attempting to usurp the power of another individual. Please understand that the husband is head of the home. His wife, according to the Word of God, is supposed to submit to him. Howbeit, this does not relinquish the woman of her power and authority. It simply means that he (the husband) is supposed to lead her (the wife) in Christ. He's not supposed to control her members (limbs), mind, will, or emotions. He's supposed to follow Christ and compel his wife to do the same. He's supposed to take authority over every ungodly thing that attempts to enter his household. He's supposed to counsel and instruct his wife in the things of God. This means that he's supposed to be saved and be fully led by the Spirit of God.

An abusive man wants to be all-powerful in regards to his wife or lover. He wants to possess every electron of her power and this is illegal, meaning, he is attempting to usurp her power. This is the evidence that the man in question has the Jezebel spirit.

When a woman keeps attracting abusive men to herself, it is because she is not fully submitted to God; then again, she may be a prophetess operating under the Ahab spirit. In other words, she possesses power that she is not utilizing. When she is under attack, she does not use her ability to bind the enemy and loose the power of God against the enemy's camp. She allows others to control and manipulate her and she is too afraid to offend them. Remember, Jezebel hates the prophets of God and is attracted to them, but when a prophet begins to fully walk in the power, authority and dominion that God has given her (or him), that prophet will not find herself (or himself) unequally yoked with the Jezebel spirit. Jezebel will be drawn to the prophet, but will not possess the ability to bind the prophet through ungodly soul ties ... especially romantic ones. When Jezebel can't unequally yoke itself using a romantic soul tie, it will often try to bind the prophet using a religious soul tie, meaning, it'll try to link the prophet up with false prophets and apostles. When a prophet of God is not guarded in the area of romance and is walking in the fear of being hurt, the fear of being abandoned, the fear of being cheated on or any fear in regards to romance, that prophet will attract a Jezebel impersonating a life's mate. When Jezebel enters that prophet's life, he or she will attempt to usurp the power of the prophet using manipulation through words and fear. Therefore, if a woman finds herself constantly attracting abusive men, it is only because she is walking in the spirit of fear and is not utilizing her God-given ability to bind and loose. If you don't bind the enemy, he will bind you. If you don't loose yourself from the enemy, he will use you to bind others. If you don't loose the power of God from within you, the enemy will come in and loose his powers against you using your own authority.

To understand this better, we need to understand the science behind power. Everything in the universe is made up of atoms. According to dictionary.com, an atom (physics) is: *the smallest component of an element having the chemical properties of the element, consisting of a nucleus containing combinations of neutrons and protons and one or more electrons bound to the nucleus by electrical attraction; the number of protons determines the identity of the element.*

Atoms are referred to as the building blocks of life. Every atom has electrons. According to Google, an electron is: *a stable subatomic particle with a charge of negative electricity, found in all atoms and acting as the primary carrier of electricity in solids.*

Electricity is the flow of electrons from one atom to another. In other words, everything in the earth has the ability to power something and every person in the earth has the ability to empower someone. This is called an electric current. Electrons can move through everything ... somethings more than others. Anything an electron can easily flow through is referred to as a conductor. A conductor has the ability to transfer power from within itself to another object. This means that we, as people, are conductors. We have the ability to move things and people. Additionally, God has given us power in the realm of the spirit to tread on the enemy. When we don't utilize this power, we begin to walk in rebellion because we are making the blood of Jesus of non-effect in our lives.

Anything that does not allow electrons to move well is called an insulator. For this reason, an insulator does not conduct electricity and does not possess much or any power. As believers, we have power that has been given to us through the Holy Spirit of God. When we do not walk in that power, we grieve the Holy Spirit. In other words, many powerful believers do not allow God to move in and through them, and therefore, they become insulators. Google defines the word "insulator" as: *a substance that does not readily allow the passage of heat or sound.* When we utilize the power of God, we use our ability to speak and bind the enemy. When we disallow the power of God from moving through us, we become dormant vessels of power with no knowledge of how to conduct the power that is within us. This is what attracts the Jezebel spirit to us. She wants to utilize our abilities to bind and loose, but she wants to pervert those abilities and unleash them against the Kingdom of God. For this reason, a fearful believer will always be used as a conduit for the kingdom of darkness.

Another way to attract the Jezebel spirit is through people bondage. When we fear offending, losing or provoking people, we will attract the Jezebel spirit to ourselves. A person who is in people-bondage will be stalked by the Jezebel spirit because that person has power that he or she is not utilizing. Jezebel wants to walk in unused power or pervert the believer so that she can use that believer's power for herself. For example, let's create a character named Mark. Mark's mother has the Jezebel spirit and she's been robbing him of his authority ever since he was a little boy. When Mark was young, his mother controlled him by threatening to beat him or take away something he loved. When Mark grew up and moved out of her house, she could no longer threaten him physically, nor could she threaten to take something away from him, so she started threatening to take someone away from him. Who is that someone? Herself, of course.

You see, Mark's mother is older and even though she has been a horrible mother to Mark, she knows that her son loves her and wants to gain her approval. Mark has not yet accepted the condition of his mother, therefore, he is ignorant of what her condition leads her to do. For this reason, he works tirelessly to please her, but whenever he attempts to walk in his own authority, Mark's mother threatens to disassociate herself from him or she pretends to be sick. She knows that one of Mark's greatest fears is that he'll hurt, shock or disappoint her so bad that she'll have a heart attack. For this reason, Mark treads softly with his mother ... even at the expense of his marriage. What Mark doesn't realize is that there is a demon operating in and through his mother to control him. Nevertheless, Mark tires himself out physically, emotionally, spiritually and financially while trying to appease a spirit that cannot and will not be appeased. This is a form of people bondage.

Another form of people bondage is when a person desires the approval, validation and acceptance of others to the point where that person fears non-acceptance. This is common today. For example, let's create a character named Joseph. Joseph is an honor student who's just been transferred to a new school. He is in the eighth grade and is in a time of his life where peer pressure is at its peak. In Joseph's new school, he notices that out of the twenty-two boys in his classroom, he is one of three boys on the honor roll. The other two boys are harassed, bullied, mocked and attacked by the ones who aren't doing so well. Additionally, most of the girls in the classroom are attracted to the "bad boys," but they are not attracted to Joseph and the other two honorees. Because of this, Joseph stops turning in his homework and he intentionally begins to fail his classes. He's trading good grades and a bright future for peer acceptance. Again, this is not uncommon.

The boys who are harassing and bullying Joseph and the

other male honorees are operating in the Jezebel spirit. They are attempting to control him through fear and intimidation. What do they want? They want Joseph to be like themselves. They want him to fail. This is how the Jezebel spirit operates. If Joseph does not mature and get delivered from his people-pleasing spirit, he will find himself being followed, bullied by and dominated by the Jezebel spirit for the rest of his life. He will likely find himself working for someone who has the Jezebel spirit, being married to someone who has the Jezebel spirit, being bullied by his own children or he will find himself operating in the Jezebel spirit.

When the Jezebel spirit stalked me, it was because I was far too passive *and* because I was rebellious. When I found myself in an abusive marriage, I feared losing the man who was abusing me. I'd sinned to get him, so I had to sin to keep him. When I started getting closer to God, I began to sin less because I loved God more. The more I submitted myself to God, the worse the abuse became. When I divorced my abusive husband, I feared marrying another man like him, so I married someone who I felt was his polar opposite. I went back into sin to get what I wanted. My second husband (we'll call him Roger) wasn't dominant at all, but he was being dominated by a family member. That family member (we'll call her Mara) then attempted to control me through him and when she could not control me, she turned to outright witchcraft.

One day, Roger went to visit Mara (she lived in a different state from us), but I didn't go. I knew what the Jezebel spirit was by then and I knew that Mara was possessed or influenced by the Jezebel spirit so I opted to stay at home. I was aware of her condition, so I was not ignorant of what her condition led her to do. She had a very strong witchcraft spirit and she usurped the authority of *everyone* who allowed her in their lives. She hated anyone who did not, as she would put it, "listen" to her. In other words, if a person did not do what she said to do, she would work tirelessly to bring that person into submission, destroy that person or destroy that person's marriage. She was well-known throughout the family for her bold and intrusive behaviors.

When Roger called me from her house, we were still married and he was simply visiting her. I was at odds with her and she was at odds with me and that's why I didn't go with him. While I was speaking with Roger over the phone, she demanded that he let her speak with me and he refused. I'd already told him that I knew she was going to ask to speak with me and I didn't want to talk with her. *By that time, I hadn't directly spoken with her in years and I wanted to keep it that way.* Because of my history with her, I knew that she would only utilize that opportunity to yell at me and threaten to destroy my marriage if I didn't "listen" to her. When Roger refused to let her speak with me, she began to yell in the background. She yelled at me, "That's why you don't have children! I put a curse on you so you wouldn't have children!" I couldn't believe what I was hearing. I had always told Roger that she was in witchcraft and he would always say that she wasn't. Eventually, she couldn't hide what she was anymore and she became more and more obsessed with controlling people. Roger would always receive calls from family members and friends about something she'd done ... almost weekly, nevertheless, he was in full submission to her. He felt like he owed her something, so he *tolerated* her behavior even when it worked against him.

At that time, I questioned why I kept coming in contact with people who were obsessed with controlling me. What I didn't realize was ... it wasn't about *me* per se. Jezebel didn't come after me so strongly because of who I am; it came after me because I didn't recognize who I am. I didn't understand the power and authority that God had given me. Jezebel came to steal the power that I wasn't using. The more I submitted myself to God, the bolder I got. This didn't stop Jezebel from coming after me; it simply changed that spirit's approach.

I came out of rebellion and I stopped tolerating dominant, controlling people. I started submitting myself to
the man I was married to, even though he wasn't saved
and God used my submission to him to deliver me from
him. At the same time, I came to understand that anytime you come between a Jezebel and her Ahab or
someone she's trying to ahab, you will find yourself in a
heated battle with Jezebel. Jezebel is a merciless spirit
who will deploy all of her powers of witchcraft against
anyone who comes between her and her Ahab.

When I stopped tolerating dominant Jezebels, the enemy started sending passive Jezebels after me. I had a set
of beliefs and reservations that opened the door for the
Jezebel spirit, even after I submitted myself to God and
began to walk in the authority that He has provided for
me through His Holy Spirit. I didn't like hurting people's
feelings and I didn't want to ever be seen as controlling
or dominant, so I tolerated behaviors that I should not
have tolerated.

Revelation 2:20 (ESV): *But I have this against you, that
you tolerate that woman Jezebel, who calls herself a
prophetess and is teaching and seducing my servants to
practice sexual immorality and to eat food sacrificed to
idols.*

As I grew in the Lord, I became aware of my dominant

friends and one by one, I started closing the doors on them by walking in authority. I started "going off" anytime they tried to control me and I began to do the opposite of what they wanted me to do. *I took my authority back.* Don't get me wrong; I was never a *push-over*, but I did allow myself to be manipulated through my own set of self-imposed rules. I stopped allowing my friends to control me with their emotions, their pity stories or their silent treatments.

Once I recognized that I was dealing with a demonic spirit, I started walking in authority against it. But the enemy, being the crafty serpent that he was, knew that I had a limited understanding in regards to the Jezebel spirit. He knew that I thought all Jezebels were dominant. I didn't realize that some Jezebels are passive and they don't use the spirit of dominance to control people; they use what I call passive manipulation.

I started being approached by passive personalities. They came off as sweet young women in need of guidance or a friend. I wasn't young in the faith anymore, but I was immature in ministry. There was a lot I didn't know (and still don't) and there was a lot I had to learn regarding the Jezebel spirit (and still do).

I would intentionally go out of my way to *not* make any

new friends. I became extremely guarded because I was tired of making friends only to have to be delivered from them. I was tired of dealing with crafty, manipulative women who saw me as nothing but one of their personal tools. I realized that people were coming into my life and using my own "rules" to manipulate and control me. So I got rid of the rules and began to walk in the authority God had given me and this became easier when my confidence began to grow in the Lord. I also began to grow confident within myself, believing that I could discern a Jezebel from a mile away. God allowed me to be humbled by allowing me to meet women who looked and sounded like they wanted godly counsel. Some of the women were in ministry; some were not. In each case, the woman would reach out to me for business or to ask me a ministry-related question. They would always ask for my phone number to further discuss whatever it was they wanted. I would give it to them and that's when Jezebel would begin to entangle me in her web.

I'd find myself ministering to what sounded like and appeared to be a sweet soul in need of help. They would ask a lot of questions; there were so many questions that they would always need to speak with me more after each call. No call was *ever* enough. They would then appeal to a need that I had; for example, they'd ask me about my likes, dislikes and dreams. If they found a need, they'd try to make themselves useful and fill it. What was supposed to be one phone call turned into several calls ... all of which lasted several hours. Before long, I would hear those oh-so-familiar words: *"I know I haven't known you long, but I feel confident enough to say that you are my best friend."* There were cases where I felt convicted because I simply wanted to help the young woman, but I didn't want to get personally involved with her. Nevertheless, I would open myself up more and more and began to share my personal business with my newfound friend. Not long after that, I found myself referring to them as my friends.

As the months and years would pass, I would find myself feeling less and less in control of my own time. In the beginning of our friendships, I thought the excessive calls were because they needed me to answer more questions, but as time passed, they asked less questions and simply began to talk more. These newfound friends would call me each and everyday and want to talk for hours at a time about absolutely nothing. But they *sounded* meek and *appeared* to be babes in Christ. I knew that I was too old (spiritually speaking) to have the friendships with them that I had because I would often find myself talking to them about things that they did not understand. I was always pouring out, but rarely (if ever) being poured into. They would always need me and I felt compelled to be there when they needed me. My time became their time and they would call me for every *little* thing. Nevertheless, I noticed that if I called them, they would rarely answer their phones so I stopped calling them altogether.

I remember the Lord kept dealing with me regarding a friend whose abusive behaviors I kept tolerating. Even though she rarely did this, the friend in question would suddenly need to consecrate whenever I offended her. *Of course, she rarely did this because I rarely offended her. We got along most of the time and that's why I tolerated those behaviors for so long.* The first time she'd done this was a day that I'd refused to fast with her. Her church was hosting a fast and because I didn't know the spirit behind the fast, nor did I know the spirit behind her church, I knew to avoid entering that fast. I didn't even know what they were fasting for, after all, we lived in different states. I prayed about it like I told her I would and the Lord responded by telling me to not enter that fast. When I told her that the Lord said no, the line suddenly went silent. Moments later, she spoke up and told me that she wouldn't be able to talk with me that week because she'd be consecrating. I felt like this was her attempt to "punish me" for not fasting with her, but since she was planning to fast anyway, I dismissed my thoughts. Howbeit, she reactivated her Facebook page a few days later. I didn't know this until I was scrolling down my timeline and noticed that she was back on and talking with everyone but me. Now, don't get me wrong. I wasn't bothered by her not talking with me because truthfully, I was able to get more work done when she "consecrated," but I have a passionate disdain for control and manipulation. I'd dealt with those spirits many times and I was determined to never deal with them again. I had always told her that I could not and would never tolerate people who didn't respect my ability to say "no." I'd always dealt with dominant people who would argue with me for saying "no," but she wasn't dominant. She wouldn't argue whenever I said "no". Instead, she would tell me that she'd be consecrating and wouldn't be making or taking any calls for a week or more.

One day, the Lord said to me, "Don't take anything off a woman that you wouldn't take off a man." God was using my own rules to help me to see that I was being mistreated. The friend was passive; she wasn't dominant at all, and that's why I refused to believe she had the Jezebel spirit or accept that her ways were jezebellic and abusive. We often think that abuse is someone hitting another person, but abusive people aren't always physically abusive, nor are they always verbally abusive.

Sometimes, they use warfare tactics to get what they want from the people they are attempting to control. For example, I was once married to an abusive man, but he didn't attack me often. Oftentimes, he'd go anywhere between one to six months without physically attacking me, but he rarely went a day without emotionally manipulating me. One of his *punishments* for me not doing something he wanted me to do or offending him in any way was him suddenly taking off and being gone for a few hours to an entire day. I've met women who were physically abused daily, so while married to him, it actually took me years to realize that I was being abused. That's because, like most abused women, I had my own definition of abuse and somehow, I managed to even convince myself that the physical abuse wasn't actual abuse. To me, we were fighting and he was winning. The more I grew in the Lord, the more I realized that he didn't use war (physical abuse) as much as he used warfare (strategies). After we separated, I created a mental list of red flag behaviors to look out for when dealing with the opposite sex. I inwardly vowed to not tolerate those behaviors from any more men. So, when I found myself tolerating those behaviors from women, I didn't think too much about it because my rules were designed to protect me in the romance arena; they were designed to help me avoid marrying another abusive man. So when the Lord told me to not tolerate from a woman what I would not tolerate from a man, He was trying to get me to wake up and realize that I was once again, allowing myself to be mistreated. I was, once again, tolerating Jezebel. It was hard for me to see this because I'm more outspoken than the friend in question. She came off as passive, sweet and harmless, plus, she was younger than I am, so I spent years in denial. Whenever I offended her, I noticed that she'd tell me that she couldn't talk with me for a week or more because she'd be consecrating. To keep me from realizing that she was indeed attempting to punish me for saying "no," she would say that she wasn't going to be talking with *anyone* for that week and she would not be on social media for a week. She would then proceed to deactivate her Facebook profile. This wasn't punishment to me because I was always busy, but I recognized that it was her *attempt* to punish me. After all, she only did this when she was offended.

One day, I was ministering to a woman who had reached out to me about a man she was courting. Whenever the guy got angry with her, he'd tell her that he was going to be consecrating for a week or more and would not be able to talk with her. I immediately recognized his behavior as abusive, demonic, and controlling, so I warned her. I told her to pull away from the guy and let God bring them back together once he'd gone through deliverance if, of course, God confirmed him to be the God-sent husband. I told her to pray about what I'd told her and she said that God had already said the very same thing to her that I was saying to her. When I got off the phone with that woman, the Lord immediately began to deal with me. He reminded me of what He'd told me regarding my friend. That's when I realized that He'd sent that woman to me so that He could use her situation to minister to me. It turned out that I was the one who was being ministered to! He suddenly reminded me of my friend's behaviors. Why did I have this rule regarding men, but I was tolerating this very same behavior from a woman I believed to be my friend? He helped me to see that I was guarded with men, but I did not guard my heart with my friends because I didn't think they could hurt me as much as a man could. The Lord started helping me to understand that guarding one's heart, as He told us to do in Proverbs 4:23, is something that has to be done with both genders. I was right to acknowledge that the behaviors were demonic and abusive, but I was wrong to only apply that knowledge to one area of my life.

During her last consecration tantrum, I noticed that my friend had reactivated her Facebook page (once again) and proceeded to talk with everyone but me. She'd done this in the past and I'd waited a few days before confronting her, but of course, when I did confront her, she would always dismiss her actions by saying she'd simply broken her fast. Nevertheless, I decided to not confront her about it again. It was time to acknowledge that I was once again dealing with the spirits of control and manipulation. I decided to close that door once and for all.

Now, here's where we shift gears. Here's where the moral of the story suddenly changes and the good guy becomes the bad guy. I could tell you many wicked things that particular friend did to me. I could go on to tell you a lot of stories about the abuse I endured while married. I could even tell you many of the things I endured when married a second time. I could point out all of the times where I'd been victimized, traumatized and penalized for my choice to say "no" to someone. I could share many testimonies with you, all the while, never assuming the blame for anything. Howbeit, if I did that, this book would be ineffective in helping anyone get delivered from Jezebel's fangs. How so? Jezebel loves victims. When I pitied myself and thought like a victim, I kept running into a new Jezebel while trying to get away from an old one. This cycle kept repeating itself time and time again until God opened my eyes and showed me that I was the common denominator in every wrong thing that happened to the adult me. Let me explain.

I have a burn on my left arm that extends almost the entire length of my arm. When my left palm is turned downward, the burn is difficult to see, but when I turn my palm upward, the burn is very visible. I got this burn when I was a curious two year old girl determined to get my hands on some peach cobbler that my mom was making. According to my mom, she'd just taken the pot of peaches off the stove and placed it on the kitchen table. She'd turned her back for a few seconds, only to turn around and see me pulling the pot towards me. It was a pot of boiling hot peaches and sugar. Before she could reach me, I'd successfully pulled the pot down and the boiling water spilled onto my left arm and the left side of my abdomen. I was severely burned and had to be rushed to the hospital. Thankfully, this happened when I was just two years old, so my skin wasn't finished growing yet. I don't have any raised burns; my skin is consistent and smooth, even where the burn marks are. Nevertheless, I got burned because I pulled down a pot of peaches. Who's to blame for that? My mom was. Now, this doesn't mean that she was a bad mother; she'd just made a bad judgment call as all mothers do. She's to blame because I was only two years old at the time. I didn't understand the concept of "hot, " and obviously, the pot was within my reach.

My mom went on to tell me another story about my

childhood. This time, I was between the ages of four and five years old and I was infatuated with insects and reptiles. I was a fearless little girl who would pick up anything that crawled, ran, rolled, flew or slithered by me (except bees and wasps). My mom said that I was standing on one of the couches in our living room while she was sweeping the floor one day. Suddenly, she swept under the other couch and to her surprise, out came a snake. She'd swept a snake from under the couch. She said that her first instinct was to look at me because she knew that I loved to catch earthworms. She knew that I would assume that the snake was actually a big worm. Not surprising, I was about to leap from the couch to go after the snake, so my mom caught me before my legs could hit the floor. Of course, she had to deal with me before she could proceed to deal with the snake. She ended up beating the snake to death with the broom. Now, had I run up to that snake and gotten bitten, whose fault would it have been? My mom would have had to assume the blame once again because I was young and she was my caretaker. She did the right thing when she saw the snake. Instead of panicking and trying to kill the snake immediately, she needed to utilize the fear she'd already instilled in me (the fear of getting a spanking) *because I obviously wasn't afraid of the snake*, to get me to stay put. After that, she was able to deal with the snake.

Before I got married the first time, my mother told me not to marry the man I was about to marry. She told me this many times, including on my wedding day. Nevertheless, I was 24 years old and I wouldn't listen. I ended up enduring a lot in that seven year marriage, and there were times when I could have lost my life. Whose fault is that? It's mine, of course! When I was a child, my mom was responsible for me, but when I became a woman, I became responsible for my own choices. This isn't to say that he wasn't responsible for his wrongdoings, but it is to say that I placed myself at his mercy. I didn't listen to God and I didn't listen to my mom, so I have to assume the responsibility for everything that happened to the adult me.

The point is ... I was a grown woman when I became friends with the woman I'd spoken of. I was a grown woman when I married my exes. I was a grown woman when I'd endured many of the things I've endured in my life. I was operating under the Ahab spirit and ever since God delivered me from that spirit, He's taught me to take responsibility for my own wrongs. Without Ahab, there wouldn't be a Jezebel. Sure, I was stalked by the Jezebel spirit, but that's because I was operating under an Ahab spirit.

When people are taught to see themselves as victims,

they will continue to be victims, but when we start taking responsibility for the consequences of *our* bad choices, we start making better choices. I've learned that true deliverance starts with confession and self-evaluation. I have a lot of stories because I've lived a pretty wonderful life. I didn't live a safe life; I took chances and I dealt with the consequences as they came. I don't regret my life at all. The only regret I have is disappointing God the many times that I did and I regret hurting the many people I've hurt. Nevertheless, if I had never fallen, I wouldn't appreciate my ability to stand. If I had never experienced the rain, I wouldn't have learned to appreciate both the sunshine *and* the rain. If I had never been attacked by the Jezebel spirit, I would not have been delivered from the Ahab spirit.

Jezebel wasn't stalking me (per se); I'd left a trail of untapped authority and Jezebel was simply following that trail. I had to recognize the patterns in my life in order for me to break those patterns. I had to break those strongholds, bind the spirits and start walking in my God-given authority before I was able to defeat the Jezebel spirit. One of the greatest lessons I've learned about that spirit is that it isn't always dominant, just as Ahab isn't always passive. I was operating as an Ahab because I feared becoming what others had been to me. I feared hurting others. This is people bondage and

Jezebel took advantage of it. I didn't want to admit to being ahab'ed ... especially being ahab'ed by a couple of babes in Christ, but I had to humble myself and acknowledge that I'd let my time and peace be controlled. I had to accept the truth to receive my deliverance. I learned that Jezebel wants to control others and she doesn't always have to be dominant to do so. Sometimes, Jezebel controls people through passive manipulation. Sometimes, Jezebel operates as a time-wasting spirit.

I didn't know how to test a spirit. I was a little too on the extreme side. I was always being led astray by my emotions and my fantasies. Had I tested the spirits of some of the people I met, I would not have spent so many years in bondage. I should have focused on everything; that way, I could look at all of the fruit in my friends' lives as well as my own. If I had opened my eyes, I would have clearly saw the Ahab spirit operating in my life. Understand this: Ahab isn't always fearful of physical or spiritual harm. I didn't fear my former friends in any way. My fear was hurting them and becoming to them what others had been to me. Again, I'd bound myself with a bunch of self-imposed rules and those rules became laws in my life. Where there are rules, there are people who are afraid to break those rules. I'd created a set of rules that I was afraid to break. This means that my former friends weren't the villains and neither was I. We were just broken souls who found each other and built friendships out of our dysfunction. The same goes for my exes. What was in them was drawn to what was in me. We all needed deliverance. Truthfully, God taught me to take myself through deliverance and when I bound up Jezebel, Ahab and every spirit under the Baal principality, I started seeing the spiritual side of my friendships and that's when I got rid of the rules and started closing doors.

If you think that Jezebel is stalking you; you may be right, however, the question is: *where is your untapped authority?* Sometimes, we can be too nice and some-times, we can be too quiet. Understand this ... a quiet vessel is an insulator. That person is disallowing the voice and the power of God from moving in and through him or her. When I realized I was being stalked, pur-sued, seduced, controlled and attacked by Jezebel, I started opening my mouth against that thing. I went into my prayer closet and I began to bind that spirit.

During my last conversation with my former friend, I suddenly received a revelation while in the middle of re-buking her. I'd been quiet with her for years, tolerating a lot of behaviors that I should not have tolerated. At that moment, it hit me: she *appeared* to be a passive, sweet young lady who couldn't hurt a fly. Most people who knew me knew I walked in authority. I'd began to not only mature in the Lord, but I started maturing in ministry. How easy would it be for me to appear to be a dominant, controlling Jezebel when dealing with a babe in Christ? I'd never dominated any of my friends or attempted to dominate them, but I learned in that moment that a friendship has to be *equally* yoked if it is to be godly. A mature Christian could not befriend a babe in Christ because if the mature Christian ever rebukes the babe, it could easily backfire. How so? Whenever you become friends with a person, you pretty much lose your ability to minister to them at a certain level. They can take *some* advice from you, but because of familiarity, they will not respect your advice. Additionally, if you rebuke them, they can use the fact that they're babes to make you look like a monster. I remember advising that particular friend many times and she couldn't seem to hear anything I'd said. She would come back to me hours, days, or weeks later and tell me the advice someone else had given her. It was the same advice (word for word) that I had given her! This happened ninety-eight percent of the time when I'd advised her! Of course, this was offensive to me ... not because she was praising another person for their advice; I could care less about that. I was offended because I realized I was talking and she wasn't listening; she was *truly* wasting my time! It was either that or she didn't want to credit me for the advice because of her intentions toward me. Either way, she was wasting my time. She'd grown familiar with me and therefore, could not receive much from me. I realized that I was on the phone to listen, but not speak. When I would speak, she would acknowledge that she heard the sound of my voice by saying, "Yeah" or "Ummhmmm" but she'd go back to speaking and everything I'd said had fallen on deaf ears. For years, I wouldn't rebuke or correct her because of my self-imposed rules. Truthfully, I felt like she was too fragile to withstand a rebuke even when I'd witnessed her doing some really shady things. I recognized the level of authority I had, so I would always be careful with her. When the Lord warned me about that friend, I wouldn't listen because of my rules. I kept passing His voice off as my own inside voice because what He was saying conflicted with what I believed, but when I finally surrendered to God in the area of friendship, I stopped tolerating her behaviors. I started rebuking her when she did wrong, but I was still being delivered from my rules, so I would try rebuking her in a friendly tone. The more God opened my eyes, the more I realized that I was being controlled. I realized that I'd been looking for dominance and trying to avoid dominant women, when the woman on the other end of the phone line was passively controlling me using my own rules against me. When I finally obeyed God and rebuked her outside of my rules, she commented about how people were always trying to control her. I had never tried to control her in all the years I'd known her and she knew this. As a matter of fact, over the years, we had always commented on how nice it was to deal with each other because we weren't controlling towards one another. However, in that moment, I realized that because I was rebuking her, she was responding to that rebuke by indirectly threatening to label me with the very spirit she knew I despised, preached against and worked tirelessly to avoid. The day that I got delivered from my rules was the day I got delivered from that friendship. That was the day that she said she'd be consecrating and could not speak with me for a week (once again) and that was the day that I washed my hands of that friendship. This isn't an indictment against her because we both needed deliverance, but the point is ... Jezebel is not always dominant and Ahab is not always passive. Truthfully, Ahab is more to blame for Jezebel's behaviors because Jezebel only does what she's allowed to do.

When you give advice to a friend who cannot receive it because of familiarity, that friendship has already started to work against you. You become the equivalent of a tape recorder, whereas, you are allowed to hear what they are saying and even play it back to them, but saying anything outside of what they want to hear renders you a voice speaking in the wilderness. When the friend is a babe in Christ, you can't really rebuke them without coming off as being dominant or controlling. This means you become nothing but a listener and a controlled speaker. The babe can easily use their position or others' perceptions of them to paint a picture of you that is not true. This revelation has since helped me as a minister to not judge other leaders who others have spoken against. I no longer side with the passive party; I've learned to pray about all things and let God show me who's who.

Understand this: Jezebels are time-consumers or time-controllers. Anytime you have a person in your life who needs large chunks of your time ... especially when most of their conversations are pointless or fruitless, your time is being controlled by the Jezebel spirit. If you do not speak up and take your time back, you will look back and realize that you've wasted a lot of time speaking when no one could actually hear you. Jezebel stalks God's prophets; that's a given. But if you want to change things and start chasing Jezebel, you have to get fully delivered from the spirit of fear. You have to renounce Ahab, come from under the Baal principality and learn to tap into the authority that God has provided for you.

CHAPTER 7

Jezebel's Favorite Masks

One of the lessons I had to learn was that Jezebel has many faces. I was always looking for certain characteristics that are commonly taught about, but I didn't realize that there was more to Jezebel than what I knew. For this reason, the Jezebel spirit was able to operate undetected in my life for years. I spent so much time trying to do the right thing that I unintentionally began to hide the truth from myself. I helped Jezebel to hide in my life. I spent so much time looking at and into myself that I failed to test the spirits in others. I didn't start identifying the hidden Jezebels in my life until I got into deliverance ministry. It was then that I found myself having to do more research regarding demonic spirits and it was then that I came to understand that Jezebel wears many masks ... many of which the traditional church does not talk about.

These faces include, but are not limited to:

- Jezebel: The Pharaoh
- Jezebel: The Parent
- Jezebel: The Spouse

- Jezebel: The In-Law
- Jezebel: The Controller
- Jezebel: The Giver
- Jezebel: The Madam
- Jezebel: The Thief
- Jezebel: The False Prophet
- Jezebel: The Boss
- Jezebel: The Protective Predator

Jezebel: The Pharaoh

How many times have you tried to get away from the Jezebel spirit, only to find yourself linked up to another Jezebel? How many times have you prayed and asked the Lord to deliver you from the Jezebel spirit, only to find yourself constantly being attacked by it? If you are like many believers, you've fought, prayed, fasted, and cried out for your freedom. Why didn't God set you free? The answer is: He did. You just needed to walk away. Let me explain.

In the story of Moses versus Pharaoh (good versus darkness), God used Moses to confront Pharaoh. The Egyptians held the Jews in captivity for over 400 years. Of course, Pharaoh was the ruler over the Egyptians. Moses was sent by God to confront Pharaoh. He told him what God said and that was to let His people go. Pharaoh refused. Moses was a representative of the apostolic anointing. Apostles are sent by God to confront, dismantle and destroy principalities, powers and rulers.

What many don't realize is that Pharaoh was operating under what we now refer to as the Jezebel spirit. How so? He'd usurped authority over God's people. This is the trademark of the Jezebel spirit. He placed the people of God in bondage and would not let them go, regardless of how many times they prayed or cried out. Pharaoh was a merciless ruler who controlled a people who did not belong under his headship and he refused to let the people of God go freely. The Bible tells us that God hardened his heart (Exodus 9:12) and of course, we know that He did so for His glory. He wanted His people to see Him moving so their faith in Him would be restored.

Like any Jezebel spirit, the more the people of God asked to be free, the harder Pharaoh worked them. Eventually, it was God who set His people free from Pharaoh, however, they had to obey Him to get out of Egypt. The same goes for you.

Most people who complain about being stalked by Jezebel have been granted many opportunities to flee Jezebel's control but did not take those opportunities. The reason they ignored their tickets to freedom was because of familiarity, unmet expectations and ungodly soul ties. For example, some people have dealt with their jezebellic mothers' abuse and mistreatment of them for most, if not all, of their lives. God opened the way of escape for them and told them to not look back, but because of familiarity and fantasies of their mothers becoming the women they believe they have the potential to become, they did not leave when God told them to. Whenever this happens, the believer will start to waver between religiousness versus obedience. They'll religiously say that God is going to save their mothers and they are supposed to stick around to help her get saved, when this is not what God said to them. Sure, God *can* save their mothers, but that's only if they *want* to be saved and are *willing* to repent of their witchcraft. The sad reality is … not everyone wants to be saved, set free, delivered or whole. Not every mother wants to be loving towards her children; that's the sad reality. Sometimes, the struggle isn't getting her saved; the struggle is for her daughter or son to make peace with the fact that she is who she wants to be. God has given her many opportunities to repent, but she chose not to. She chose darkness over light. One of the traits of the Jezebel spirit is … people who have it are so prideful that they refuse to repent and whenever they attempt to apologize, their apologies are not authentic. Instead, they are often laced with sarcasms, blame, deflections, etc. For example, if a woman with a Jezebel spirit was to strike her 25-year-old daughter simply because her daughter respectfully offered up an opinion that was different than her own, she would likely say, "I'm sorry if you think I went too far by hitting you. I'm sorry that I'm not the mother you've always wanted. I'm sorry that your life is going the direction it is going in! Maybe when I'm dead, you can finally get some peace." This is the rantings of a Jezebel spirit. Her words are designed to ridicule, insult, demean and hurt the victim. They are also designed to help Jezebel cast herself as the victim.

Another example of an ahab'ed soul refusing to get out when God told them to get out is in the case; for example, of an abused woman. She loves her husband and wants so badly for her marriage to work. Her husband, however, has a Jezebel spirit and does not want to be free. He likes being the way that he is, but his wife refuses to accept this fact, so she works tirelessly and single-handedly to hold her marriage together. In the midst of her fighting for her marriage, she endures physical, emotional, verbal, and financial abuse. She cries out to God, begging that He save her husband and save her marriage, but God answers her in a different way. He gives her a chance to escape the man who is or has become nothing less than a weapon formed against her. She refuses to leave because of unmet expectations and ungodly soul ties. She needs to be delivered from the

Ahab spirit.

Please understand that the Jezebel spirit is a taskmaster; it is a ruler spirit that sees people as nothing but mere tools designed to be used for its own selfish gratification. When dealing with Jezebel, the Pharaoh, you will soon discover that the life you're fantasizing about having with the person bound by the Jezebel spirit is not the same life that person is fantasizing about having with you. The fighting comes in because the two of you are working to achieve conflicting results. You may be working towards peace and resolution between yourself and the person who has the Jezebel spirit, but that person is working around the clock to get you under his or her control. I've discovered that in these cases, the problem isn't getting Pharaoh to let God's servant go; the challenge is getting the believer to believe God and utilize the way of escape He has provided for him or her. Many believers are standing in front of their own personal Red Seas, still trying to convince Pharaoh to come with them.

Jezebel: The Parent
As mentioned in the previous pointer, all too often, believers find themselves in the grips of a jezebellic parent. In most cases when this happens, the believer works tirelessly to get that parent saved. I've witnessed

many cases where believers have even searched for deliverance ministers in hopes that if they found someone who could cast the devil out of their mothers or fathers that they would finally have the relationships with them that they wanted. Here's the problem with this. The parent does not want to be free and is not aware of their daughter or son's attempt to get them into a deliverance ministry. This is also very similar to an abused woman trying to drag her husband to a deliverance ministry, hoping that he'll get delivered and stop abusing her. This doesn't happen. The reasons this doesn't happen includes:

- God won't force deliverance on someone who doesn't want it.
- Jezebels have trouble repenting ... especially when they are not truly sorry.
- To get delivered, the person must first relinquish all of his or her ungodly fantasies and expectations. Understand this: whatever it is that Jezebel has had them fantasizing about has become something they have been investing in. Telling a person bound by the Jezebel spirit to relinquish his (or her) dreams is similar to telling a person who's been building a house for 32 years to abandon the project ... even though they think the project is almost complete.
- Power, in itself, can be addictive, so most people

who have operated as dominating, controlling Jezebels are addicted to the power they have over others. They like the way power feels and they like the benefits they believe they get from controlling others. Now, this is their belief system *outside* of the Jezebel spirit. This means that they actually like how they are.

- Even after deliverance, the person has to maintain his or her freedom.
- A person must want deliverance for himself or herself. We can't want something for someone more than that person wants it for himself or herself.

Jezebellic parents often start breaking their children from the moment they are born. When their children are young, they will often use physical abuse, verbal abuse, toys, money and relatives to control the children. Jezebel's children often fear her, but at the same time, they wrestle with the Jezebel spirit, the Ahab spirit or the eunuch spirit.

Jezebel often uses a child's need to feel loved and accepted by his or her parent to her advantage. Children born to Jezebel will often feel starved of love. Jezebel does this so that she can use love as a reward for her children's obedience to her. When, for example, her daughter makes good grades and says that she's going to go to college and enter the profession her mother told her to enter, Jezebel will reward her with money, gifts or simply by being nice to her. By doing this, the mother is training her child to serve her. When her daughter does not do what she expects of her, Jezebel will punish her by spanking, abusing, yelling, or taking something away from her that she wants. She may even send her to someone else's house (namely another relative bound by the Jezebel spirit) as a punishment for not doing what she was told or expected to do.

The children of Jezebel often work tirelessly to gain their mother's approval. Anytime they see their mothers smiling, they get overly excited and believe they've earned their mother's affection or are at least close to earning it. They may strive to get good grades in school, keep their rooms clean and may even do some extra chores in an attempt to win over their mother's affection. Nevertheless, with Jezebel, good enough is never enough. Like everyone else, Jezebel's children are nothing but mere tools to help her get whatever it is that she wants.

Jezebels are often high-achievers and will push their children to do well, but this isn't because they love their children. They do this because they want to gain the respect of others. Respect, for Jezebel, equals more power and opportunities to control the people around her. When Jezebel's children do not accomplish the goals Jezebel has set for them, she will unleash a fury of words designed to break their spirit and bring them back into full submission to her. Additionally, she doesn't want them to be as successful as she is (if, of course, she is successful). The reason for this is ... Jezebel functions best in co-dependent relationships where she can give her approval and her money to her children in exchange for their submission to her.

Jezebels will oftentimes use money to control their adult children. They love to make their children dependent on them, but at the same time, they will complain about their children being dependent on them. In truth, they love knowing when their children cannot function outside of their wallets because this allows Jezebel to control her children, even when they become parents themselves. This also allows her to control her grandchildren as well as her son and/or daughter-in-laws.

When dealing with a parent who has the Jezebel spirit, the only thing a daughter or a son can do is:
1. Tell the parent about his or her behaviors and ask the parent to change.
2. Provide information to the parent about the

Jezebel spirit.

3. Refuse to tolerate the parent's ungodly behavior. If you tolerate Jezebel, that spirit will attack you viciously until it gets what it wants from you. Even then, it won't be satisfied. Know this: demons have the appetite of hell; they cannot be appeased.

4. Stay away from the parent until the parent seeks deliverance for himself or herself. Sometimes, this can take years and in some cases, sadly enough, the parent never chooses to get set free.

5. In many cases, the children of Jezebel have to distance themselves from the majority or all of their family. This is often the case when the entire family is under the witchcraft and control of Jezebel and are always saying things like:

> "She means well."

> "That's just how your mother is. Just love her like that."

> "She put clothes on your back, fed you and gave you a place to stay! How dare you question your mother!"

Jezebels often have many people in the family under their control and these people will give you what appears to be reasonable advice, but in truth, what they are really saying is: "Just let her abuse you, break you, tear down your marriage, emotionally scar your children and do whatever she feels is necessary to get what she wants from you. You, at least, owe her that much." This is not a godly response. It is the response of a person under Jezebel's witchcraft and control. This is the response of someone trying to win favor with Jezebel.

Matthew 12:46-50 (ESV): *While he was still speaking to the people, behold, his mother and his brothers stood outside, asking to speak to him. But he replied to the man who told him, "Who is my mother, and who are my brothers?" And stretching out his hand toward his disciples, he said, "Here are my mother and my brothers! For whoever does the will of my Father in heaven is my brother and sister and mother."*

Know this. Sometimes, the womb of Jezebel is the vehicle God used to get you here, but being birthed and raised by someone who has the Jezebel spirit does not mean that you owe that person anything except to love them. Some people have to be loved from a distance.

Romans 13:8 (ESV): *Owe no one anything, except to love each other, for the one who loves another has fulfilled the law.*

Matthew 12:46-50 (ESV): *While he was still speaking to the people, behold, his mother and his brothers stood outside, asking to speak to him. But he replied to the man* *who told him, "Who is my mother, and who are my brothers?" And stretching out his hand toward his disciples, he said, "Here are my mother and my brothers! For whoever does the will of my Father in heaven is my brother and sister and mother."*

Jezebel: The Spouse

Dealing with the Jezebel spirit in a marriage is one of the hardest storms to endure. The reason for this is ... spouses live together, are soul-tied, have children together, have blended their finances, and have made plans (and investments) towards a future together. So whenever we come in contact with the Jezebel spirit in a spouse, it will threaten to destroy everything you love. The worst part is ... it has access through the marriage to make good on its promises or attempt to make good on its promises.

Jezebellic spouses are very controlling, manipulative, emotional, crafty, vengeful and unpredictable. They will threaten to divorce their spouses, take the children away, and destroy everything they've worked so hard to establish if they do not get their way. They are oftentimes physically abusive and overly determined to control the people around them. One of the most common things to hear a spouse with the Jezebel spirit say is, "If you would've listened to me, this wouldn't have happened." I've discovered that with Jezebel, the word "listen" is synonymous with "obey me."

I've endured a physically abusive marriage and up until recently, I didn't realize that the man I was married to had the Jezebel spirit. The reason for this is ... I didn't know what the Jezebel spirit was back then. I just thought he was a nice guy who didn't know how to manage his emotions when he got angry. Like most abuse victims, I focused on the good side of him, working tirelessly to help him understand that he didn't need to scream at me, punish me, threaten me, or physically attack me. Nevertheless, being the babe that I was, I wasn't exactly a model spouse either. I was determined to not do whatever it was that he said do whenever he became angry. I would intentionally go left if he said to go right because I didn't want to be controlled. This entails that I too was wrestling with the Jezebel spirit. One of the things I've learned is that Ahabs are usually Jezebels in training.

Like most women in abusive marriages, I saw my husband as two people. I saw the wonderful man I'd fallen in love with and I was determined to hold on to him. Then again, I saw the monster he'd become whenever we had a difference of opinion. So I tried to get rid of the monster by appealing to the man when he wasn't angry.

This would only cause the Jezebel spirit to manifest in him.

When married to Jezebel, a spouse will find himself or herself always trying to single-handedly save the very marriage that their spouses are threatening to destroy. I've come across many abused men and women and their stories all read the same way mine read. A Jezebel-lic spouse will always use their partners' love for them as a weapon against them. Why is this? Because Satan hates love, after all, God is love. You have to understand that it isn't necessarily the spouse who's threatening the marriage. All too often, when this happens, the Jezebel spirit in the spouse is manifesting and provoking the spouse to go to the extremes in an attempt to get their way.

Jezebels tend to:

- threaten to leave their spouses when upset.
- remove their house keys from their key rings or threaten to take their names off the lease (if you are leasing an apartment or house with them).
- remove their wedding rings ... sometimes, threatening to throw them away or actually throwing them. This is an attempt to upset the ahab'ed spouse and show the spouse how far they are willing to go to get what they want.
- talk favorably about previous lovers. This is an

attempt to make the ahab'ed spouse feel *lucky* or *blessed* to have them. This is also a passive-aggressive threat, whereas, the jezebellic spouse is pretty much threatening to reconcile with their former lovers should their marriages fail.

* collect and hold on to embarrassing photos, damning text messages or anything they feel they can use to get the upper hand in an argument or in court ... should the marriage not work. They love to use those text messages and notes to upset themselves whenever they have another argument with their spouses. They do this to justify their over-the-top reactions to small offenses. For example, if the jezebellic spouse becomes angry with the ahab'ed spouse for not spending as much money on him as he spent on her for Valentine's day, he will open an old text message from her that she sent several weeks or months ago during a heated argument. He will then use that text message to justify escalating the argument. He may say, for example, "Three weeks before Christmas, you text messaged me and told me that you were going to leave me. You told me that you didn't feel the same way about me like you used to feel. I thought we'd worked past that, but this gift proves to me that you meant every word you said." This is Jezebel's attempt to cast

himself as the victim and justify the attack he is about to inflict on his ahab'ed lover.

- manipulate their spouses into disassociating from any friends or family members who do not agree with Jezebel's agenda. This is done to separate the ahab'ed spouse from anyone who loves them and has the ability to encourage or uplift them. This is also done to starve the spouse of love; that way, the spouse will mistake what Jezebel is giving them for love.

- deprive their spouses of sex when angry or reward their spouses with sex whenever they get what they want.

- have angry, quick or emotional sex with their spouses in an attempt to make the spouse feel worthless, or they may request sexual favors that make the ahab'ed spouse feel cheap and unappreciated. Most of these "favor requests" will be favors they know their spouses will refuse to do because of how demeaning they are. If and when the spouse refuses, the jezebellic spouse will inflict a greater punishment on the ahab'ed spouse.

- leave their homes for hours and days at a time in an attempt to *punish* their spouses for not complying with their demands. Jezebels love to terrorize their lovers because fear, again, is synonymous with Ahab. The more fear the victim feels, the stronger the Ahab spirit will be in that person.

- say things like, "I'm getting really tired" or "To tell you the truth, I've already left this marriage." Remember, fear is the name of the game and Jezebel always plays to win!
- break things when they don't get their way. This is especially true for sentimental objects such as photos of the couple, gifts they've received from their spouses, gifts they've given their spouses, or anything that has sentimental value to the spouse.
- blame their spouses for their extramarital affairs by saying things like, "This happened the night you said this to me or you did that to me." This is to relinquish themselves from accepting full blame because Jezebel hates repentance.

Of course, there are many characteristics of the Jezebel in spouse-form, but the overall message here is ... they are power-thirsty, controlling, manipulative and merciless.

Jezebellic spouses are always reaching for power and they don't like the idea of their spouses having any type of power over them. For this reason, they will rarely apologize for anything and when they do apologize, they are often either being sarcastic, or they'll share the blame with the spouse. They will not assume full blame because to them, this gives the spouse too much power and they are afraid that their spouses will do the same thing that they are doing and that is ... abuse the power that they have or think they have.

The jezebellic spouse is not to assume all of the blame for the problems in the marriage. In every case where I've witnessed a spouse being controlled by another spouse, the controlled spouse was guilty of idolizing the jezebellic spouse. This idolatry alone not only opened the door for Jezebel to enter their lives, but it gave Jezebel the tools he or she needed to effectively tear down and rebuild their ahab'ed spouses.

The first few years of a Jezebel-Ahab union are the hardest because the Jezebel spirit will work tirelessly to train and gain full control over the ahab'ed spouse. This will oftentimes be done using emotional warfare, trickery and physical attacks. Nevertheless, make no mistake about it ... even if the ahab'ed spouse begins to submit to Jezebel, the jezebellic spouse will always find himself or herself reaching for more power. In other words, there is no way to satisfy such a soul because demons have the appetite of hell.

201

Jezebel: The In-law

In-laws bound and used by the Jezebel spirit aren't a huge problem *unless* you are married to someone who is under their control ... especially if the person you've married is someone they've ahab'ed. Understand this: Not everyone under Jezebel's control is an Ahab. Some people are the equivalent of eunuchs, while others serve as guards. A eunuch, according to Google is: *a man who has been castrated, especially (in the past) one employed to guard the women's living areas at an oriental court.* Google also defines eunuch as: *an ineffectual person.*

Eunuchs were castrated to ensure that they would not have sex with the queen or any of the king's concubines. They were also castrated to ensure that they remained loyal to the kingdom. People in those times understood that a married man would have children with his wife and want to be near his wife or children. Howbeit, eunuchs lived in the castle; that was their home. This was designed to ensure that the eunuch was loyal to the king and the kingdom only. Everyone else, including the eunuch's parents, were irrelevant to the eunuch.

A eunuch these days is nothing more than a person who is incapable of living without Jezebel's instructions or aid. They will often do whatever Jezebel tells them to do and in exchange, Jezebel makes them feel loved, needed, appreciated and wanted. Ahab, on the other hand, is a person who has authority but is too afraid to use that authority. Jezebels always walk and operate in Ahab's authority. Guards are nothing but people who Jezebels use as tools to accomplish their agendas. For example, a guard is that aunt who criticizes Jezebel's adult children for telling her the truth or not doing whatever it is she said to do. A guard is that in-law who calls to criticize the ahab'ed spouse for upsetting Jezebel and not doing whatever it is that Jezebel wanted them to do.

People who have been ahab'ed by a family member (oftentimes their own mothers) will feel like they are being forced to choose between Jezebel and their spouses. For this reason, they will attempt to find some balance between giving Jezebel what it wants and giving the spouse enough of themselves to keep them from complaining. For example, when I was married the second time, my then-husband (Roger) definitely had the Ahab spirit. As I mentioned earlier, he was fully under the control of one of his family members (Mara). When Roger and I first got married, Mara began to work tirelessly to get me under her control, but I refused to submit to her. Because I wouldn't submit to her, she would punish me by calling and speaking reproachfully about me to Roger, calling to criticize me for anything I did wrong ... including not answering her phone calls fast enough, talk about me to the family and give Roger advice that she knew would destroy our marriage. When I complained to Roger (in the beginning), he would become overly stressed and say things like, "I'm so confused" and "I don't know what to do to fix this." To me, the solution was simple ... I told him to get Jezebel out of our marriage and stop letting her advise him regarding me. Nevertheless, he felt like he owed her something because, as he put it, she'd helped him out a lot when he was going to school.

Jezebels love to make their family members partially or fully dependent on them either emotionally, financially or spiritually. They also establish themselves as people who will give you the shirt off their own backs if you were to need it. This is oftentimes what you'll hear Jezebel's family saying about her (or him). They will write off Jezebel's behavior by saying, "She's got her ways, but there's nothing she won't do for family" or "That's just the way she is, but underneath it all, she's really a good person." They fail to acknowledge the snarling, divisive, always upset person that Jezebel tends to be. They also fail to acknowledge the many families that Jezebel has destroyed with her conniving ways. They will always point their fingers at the people who failed to please Jezebel, pointing out the few or the many charitable acts that Jezebel has done for those people. For example, Mara flew to Europe to put her uncle's wife out of their (the couple's) own home because the uncle complained to her that his wife had loaned money to her brother without his knowledge or permission. He was really upset with his wife, so he confided in Mara. Mara then loaned him some money and bought herself a ticket to France. She said to Roger that she was going to go and pack the woman's clothes and throw her out. When she arrived in France, she tried to carry out her plans, but the uncle defended his marriage. He told her that she did not have the right to put his wife out and that the problem was a simple spat between him and his wife. He would not let her condemn or criticize the wife, so in a blind rage, Mara returned to the United States and began to turn the family against her uncle. The uncle had made two mistakes and they were: to tell Mara about his marital problems and to accept money from her. This made her feel as if she was an equal partner in the marriage and had the right to say whether the marriage failed or continued. When she realized that she did not have the power to get rid of the uncle's wife, she started trying to control how others saw the uncle. Sadly enough, she was successful at turning many of their family against him.

Anytime Jezebel has a voice in a marriage, she will use that voice of hers to control how the spouses see each other. Jezebels believe themselves to be all-powerful and anyone who Jezebel has advised, helped or fed is seen by Jezebel as nothing but personal property. They only have the rights to make their own decisions when those decisions do not conflict with Jezebel's decisions for them or opinions of them. In other words, they are mere slaves.

Jezebel: The Controller

Jezebels are controlling; we all know this, but control isn't always dominant control. Sometimes, it's passive manipulation or playful coercion. Most of us are familiar with the dominant Jezebel. As a matter of fact, most leaders who teach about the Jezebel spirit only teach about her dominant side. Nevertheless, Jezebel has many faces and many forms and it doesn't always use dominance to get what it wants.

Dominant Jezebels tend to be aggressive, loud and seemingly fearless. They control others using the mechanism of fear, humiliation (or threats of humiliation), or by threatening to take something away from a person that they want, need, value, or idolize. A good example of a dominant Jezebel is a woman who dines in at a restaurant. When her waiter comes to the table, the first thing that she does is tries to establish that she's different from his other customers. She'll ask the waiter for his name. This is the first attempt to control him. What she's doing is capturing the waiter's attention by trying to get personal with him. She will repeat his name aloud or maybe even write it down. This is a scare tactic designed to assure that the waiter gives her favorable attention. This is her way of saying, "If you don't serve me the way I want to be served, I will report you and put your job at risk." Additionally, if the waiter fears losing his job and gives Jezebel the praise and attention she wants, she will always ask to be seated in his section whenever she dines in that restaurant. She will often ask for him by name.

After she's gotten the waiter's name, she will tell him her name or title if her title is something she's proud of (example: doctor, lawyer, pastor, professor, etc.). Again, this is to establish a sense of familiarity and to distinguish herself from his other customers. She wants the waiter to esteem her and see her as important. After this, she will almost always request some dish be made differently than the restaurant normally makes it. "Don't put corn in my soup," she'll say. "And only use fresh tomatoes in my salad." She wants them to special make everything for her because Jezebel is a prideful spirit. She will even change her mind a few times. For example, she may say, "I've changed my mind about the soup. Bring me the cabbage greens, but tell the cook to use fresh cabbage and add carrots to it." This is done to establish her identity with the waiter; it is to get him to remember her because Jezebel likes to create soul ties with anyone she comes in contact with.

Jezebel will keep the waiter coming back to her table, even interrupting him as he serves other customers. If the waiter does not serve Jezebel the way she wants to be served, she will ask him to go and get his manager. She will then try to establish her identity and create some form of familiarity with the manager. That way, whenever she is in the restaurant, she can use the manager's name as a scare tactic. For example, the next time she dines in, she may ask her waitress, "Is Phil here today?" Even though she doesn't personally know Phil (the manager), she will use his name to bring the waitress into submission.

Jezebels will also try to get the cooks at their favorite restaurants under their control. This is done by getting the cook or cooks to recognize her by getting them familiar with her special requests. She'll ask the waiter, for example, "Am I the only one who asks for carrots to be put in their cabbage greens?" She's asking this question because she *wants* to be the *only* one making that request. If the waiter says that there is one other person or a few other people who request carrots in their cabbage greens, she will change her order request. Again, her goal is to get the cook or cooks familiar with her requests so that her orders can get specialized attention from them. After a few visits to that restaurant, she'll start asking the waiter things like, "Who's in the kitchen tonight?" If the cook is someone who does not fear Jezebel, she will keep sending her dishes back until the cook serves her the way she wants to be served. If the cook refuses to submit to her, she will send in a lot of complaints about that cook until the cook loses his or her job or the cook starts serving her the way she wants to be served. If the restaurant owner does not fire the cook or demand that the cook be subject to Jezebel, Jezebel will stop going to that restaurant and she'll take to the internet and leave a few bad reviews about that restaurant. Remember, if Jezebel can't control you, she'll try to control how others see you.

Jezebels love familiarizing themselves with people in authority. They do this so they can use those peoples' names in their attempts to control and scare others. For example, a small-town Jezebel can be heard saying, "All I have to do is make a few phone calls and you'll be finished in this town!" This is her way of saying that she controls the authorities in that town.

Jezebels can also be passively controlling. Passive

Jezebels are more manipulative than they are dominant. They will often link themselves to people in authority and then, they will use their prey's perception of them to get whatever it is that they want. For example, let's say that a woman named Margaret is married to a man named Trent. Margaret is passive and she appears to be harmless. Trent, on the other hand, is recognizably more assertive, even though he does not control or attempt to control his wife. Margaret knows that people see her as harmless and sweet. She also knows that if Trent does not do whatever it is that she wants him to do, she can control Trent by controlling how others see Trent.

Margaret starts appearing to be sad while at work. When her co workers ask her what the problem is, she will likely indirectly or directly point the blame at Trent. In some instances, she may tell the truth when the truth is damning. In other instances, she may lie or make implications that Trent has done something really bad to her. This is to get her co-workers to sympathize with her and feel the need to protect her from Trent.

One day, Trent grows tired of Margaret's crafty ways, so he leaves her. Upset that she can't get Trent to return home, she goes to work and implies or directly states that Trent has been abusing her. You see, people see Margaret as soft-spoken, fragile, kind and helpless, but she's far from it. Margaret is a passive or passive-aggressive Jezebel who knows how to use the heartstrings of the people around her to control the people in her life. I've had friends like this and one of the lessons I learned is ... never be friends with anyone who appears harmless when you appear to be bold and assertive. Why is this? Because Jezebel will use people's perceptions of her to her advantage. When she does not get her way or if you attempt to disassociate yourself from her, she will reach out to people she believes to be more powerful (spiritually, socially or financially) than you are (especially the people who are influential in your life) and she will imply or directly say that you've abused her in one way or another. She may imply that you controlled or attempted to control her when this is not the truth. Nevertheless, because she *appears* to be sweet, soft-spoken and introverted while you appear to be bold, assertive and extroverted, people will often believe her side of the story; that is, until they personally get to know her and she does the same thing to them. The last time I dealt with a person like this, I noticed that she kept reaching out to anyone I respected or was affiliated with. I didn't realize it at the time, but she was being strategic. She needed them to see her; she needed them to believe that she was introverted and harmless. When she reached out to Apostle Marcia (the Apostle I was serving under), what was in her could not hide. Apostle Marcia called and warned me about her, but I didn't listen because I saw the Apostle as assertive and extroverted, whereas, I saw my friend as passive and introverted. That was because I had little knowledge about the Jezebel spirit and I didn't realize, at that time, that walking in authority is not the same as being dominant.

When Jezebels use playful coercion, it is oftentimes used against the opposite sex. When a Jezebel is beautiful and she realizes that a man, for example, is so enticed by her beauty that he'll do anything to have her, she will flirt with him to get her way. To her, he is nothing but a mere tool to be used whenever needed. For example, let's say that Margaret becomes a single woman and finds herself locked out of her car. She doesn't want to shell out the $60 fee her local locksmith charges, so she calls her neighbor (Robert) to help her. She's not interested in Robert because he's not powerful enough or she knows she can't ahab him, nevertheless, she decides to flirt with him from time-to-time so that she can use him whenever possible.

Jezebels will also link themselves to violent people. Again, this is an attempt to control others. A good example is a local Jezebel who helps the troubled boys in his neighborhood. He's always taking them out to dinner, buying them gifts and acting as a father-figure in their lives. Let's say that he happens to be in ministry.

One day, Jackson (the Jezebel) discovers that another minister has been exposing some of his dishonest dealings. Because he can't control the minister or the people affiliated with the minister, he will likely turn to the troubled youth. He won't directly tell them to do anything to the minister, but he will tell them that the man is attempting to destroy his ministry or career. He will even use the power of suggestion to coerce them into attacking or threatening the guy. Please understand that the youth he has linked himself with don't know how to deal with conflict outside of violence and he knows this. He may not give them the minister's address, but he'll leave subtle clues for them so they can easily figure out where the minister stays, where the minister teaches or where the minister works. Jackson wants them to harm or maybe even kill the minister, but he wants to make sure that his hands don't get dirty in the process. He wants to remain blameless, so he won't tell them (in most cases) to do anything to the minister, but what he will do is appeal to their respect of him and need for him. To him, they are but disposable tools to be used at his discretion.

Jezebels are controllers, but always remember that each Jezebel's method of control will depend on the personality of the individual the Jezebel is in, coupled with the Jezebel's agenda. Sure, the controlling principal at your son's high school may very well have the Jezebel spirit, but at the same time, his meek music teacher may also have the Jezebel spirit. When Jezebel enters an extroverted person, it may behave in a dominant way, but when it enters an introverted person, it may use manipulation as its choice method of gaining control.

Jezebel: The Giver
Have you ever heard someone say they've gotten a new lease on life? What that person means is they have a different perspective regarding life or people than the one they initially had. However, Jezebels tend to lease the lives of people through gift-giving and charitable acts.

I've personally known people who were ahab'ed by one of their family members when I was affiliated with them. One of those people was, of course, Roger. Others were friends and family members. One of the things I noticed about the Jezebels in their lives was that they were very giving and sometimes even helpful in times of need. Honestly, the people under Jezebel's control felt like they *needed* the Jezebels in their lives ... even though they complained about their jezebellic relatives' ways. It was very similar to an abusive relationship between a husband and a wife. The Jezebels would dominate, control, intimidate, belittle, and gossip about the people they were ahab'ing. In some cases, the people dominated by Jezebel were physically attacked. In each case, I witnessed the abused party finally come to their senses for a short period of time. They'd tire of Jezebel's controlling ways and begin to share with others the abuse they'd suffered at the hands of their jezebellic relatives. They'd boldly and confidently confess that they were not going to return to Jezebel's house, nor would they have any further dealings with Jezebel. Between a week to a few months later, the abused party will have taken on a different tone. Suddenly, they are quiet about their dilemma with the Jezebel in their lives ... so much so that the people they've confided in have to inquire of them regarding the outcome of the incidents they once complained about. One of the most common responses is, "We talked." What this means is Ahab and Jezebel have reconciled and the ahab'ed party is too ashamed to talk about it. For this reason, the abused party will remain silent until they have something good to say about their abusive relative. This is to change the people's minds (once again) about Jezebel. "We talked," they can be heard saying. "She told me that she was frustrated that day when she hit me because she'd just gotten written up at work, plus, one of my cousins lied to her and told her that I said she needed help." From here, they will relinquish Jezebel of any wrongdoing and place the full blame for the incident on the cousin. After that, they will share some good deed that Jezebel has recently done for them. "She took me out to eat on Saturday," says the ahab'ed soul and she also gave me two hundred dollars to get myself some new clothes." Here, what the person is doing is trying to portray their abusive relative as good, charitable and simply misunderstood. They are painting Jezebel's eyes for her. In other words, they are trying to make her look better. Nevertheless, as soon as Jezebel attacks them again, they will have another moment of honesty where they'll tell the truth about what Jezebel has been taking them through.

Jezebels tend to buy control over their victims. In each case where I'd witnessed people being controlled by Jezebel, I saw an extreme dynamic where they were either extremely happy with Jezebel, extremely upset at Jezebel or extremely confused by Jezebel's words or ways. Jezebel is a highly-charged spirit that loves to use a person's own emotions against them. Nevertheless, to ensure that this charade is never-ending, Jezebels tend to buy gifts for their Ahabs ... sometimes even putting themselves in debt to do so. But that's no problem for Jezebel. Having power over another human being is well worth the investment. Truthfully, many Jezebels are paying monthly notes to finance the Ahabs that they are leasing. Mara had a lot of credit cards and she'd help anyone who was under her control if they asked for help. After they received money from her or a place to stay, she'd escalate her control over them and demand that they "listen" to her more. If they agreed, she'd buy them a few new gifts or give them something that she wasn't using. She would always finance her right to control people. Understand this: nothing Jezebel gives you is free. There's always a hidden agenda and a price tag attached to every little or big thing that Jezebel gives you or does for you.

Jezebel: The Madam

Some Jezebels (especially the older ones who've lost their youthful charm) tend to behave, think and reason like madams. A madam, according to dictionary.com is: *the woman in charge of a house of prostitution.* They will oftentimes suggest that a woman sleeps with a man to get what she wants or that a man sleeps with a woman to get what he wants. Jezebels always act as if your sexual organs belong to them. In some cases, they will directly suggest that the person they are ahab'ing or has ahab'ed use sex to coerce another person into a relationship or to give them something they want. In other cases, they'll hint around, but won't be so direct. For example, Roger and I had just gotten married and we'd flown to the state Mara was living in to visit her. One day, Mara started complaining about neck pains. At this time, Mara and I were in good-standing with one another. I didn't pay Mara's complaints about neck pain too much attention. I assumed she'd take a few aspirin and lie down, but to my surprise, she laid face down on the floor next to me. I was sitting on the floor watching television. "Can you massage my neck?" she asked. It's funny because I'd never had a woman to ask me for a massage before. In my family, if a woman needed a massage, she'd ask her boyfriend or husband to give it to her, and if she happened to be single, she'd simply remark that she needed a massage, but she wouldn't ask another woman for one. Honestly, the women in my family rarely asked one another for back scratches. It was not uncommon to see an aunt, for example, standing in the doorway, using the doorpost to scratch her back . I wasn't too alarmed by Mara's request, but I can honestly say that I was uncomfortable, nevertheless, I obliged.

Roger was in another room when I started massaging Mara's neck, but Mara's loud voice carried to every room in her small apartment. "Ohhh, you have good hands," she exclaimed in her thick African accent. "You can make a lot of money massaging people." Mara kept complimenting my hands and then, she told me that her boyfriend normally paid her $40 to massage him. The truth was, however, Mara didn't have an *actual* boyfriend. The guy she was talking about was not familiar with her family or vice versa. He simply came over to her apartment in the middle of the night when everyone was sleeping. He'd then leave early in the morning before anyone woke up. He didn't take her out on dates or in public, for that matter. Their relationship was restricted to Mara's house and Mara's bedroom only. Occasionally, she'd cook something and drop it off at his job, but that was it. There was no relationship. The guy was American and almost immediately, I was able to discern his character. I didn't know much about demons back then, but I knew what type of man he was. I'd met him one time while at her house and he didn't seem eager to get to know me or Roger. He made his way to her bedroom and waited on her. An hour or two later, he emerged from the bedroom, bidding us farewell.

Mara kept suggesting that I could make a lot of money and then, she told me that her *boyfriend* had a friend he was often with and she was sure he'd pay me to massage him. I knew I wasn't going to massage *anyone* except Roger (I wasn't even comfortable massaging her neck), so I countered by telling her that no man would be happy if his wife was in another room massaging another man. Mara smiled. At first, she told me that it was easy money and Roger wouldn't have a problem with it. After that, she said that we didn't have to tell Roger. "You know how men are," she said. "Sometimes, they make a big deal out of nothing." She went on to say that she could get her boyfriend's friend and maybe even a few of his friends and I could make money massaging them. I was employed full time and I'd never asked Mara for any money, so it was confusing to me as to why she was so adamant about making me a black market masseuse. I was more than shocked; I was offended and I was sure Roger had heard every word of our conversation and would be offended as well.

When I brought it to his attention, he acted as if it wasn't a big deal, but for me, I felt like she was trying to put me on the market. In street terms, I felt like she was trying to "set me out." Of course, I refused and this is one of the incidents that started our five year battle. She felt I was being stupid because I didn't want to make "easy money" as she called it and I felt like she was trying to prostitute me.

I talked with Roger about it, even though I was sure he'd overheard the conversation, but he was very nonchalant about it all. At first, he dismissed her behavior until I told him she'd even offered to loan me her bedroom (not her living room) to perform the massages. I then went on to tell him that no man was going to be in a bedroom with a woman, receiving a massage and not expect more. He responded by saying that he'd talk with her about it and that it wasn't a big deal. Mara saw how offended I was and never made that petition to me again.

I noticed that Mara did something very similar with many of the young women under her control. I would often hear her saying to her male relatives, "I have girl for you" or "If it's a girl you want, I can get one for you." To her, the women who depended on her or liked one of her relatives were nothing more than tools to accomplish her own agenda. She would often offer them up without their knowledge. I've never seen a man agree, but I always assumed that if a man were to agree to Mara's offer, she'd manipulate the women into sleeping with the guy.

Unfortunately for Mara, I'd been brought up around some shady individuals. I'd come across women like her in my young adult life, so I recognized what she was doing immediately. They were oftentimes middle-aged or older women who'd befriend a lot of younger women, gain their respect by helping them whenever they needed help and helping them out by babysitting their children. They would directly or indirectly tell the women they were helping to use sex to better their lives. For example, many of us have met that woman who was maybe ten to twenty years our senior. She sat out on her front step or the curb in front of her house everyday, smoking a cigarette and talking with some man. Occasionally, we'd see her outside talking with some distraught woman. She'd either be encouraging and hugging the woman or she'd be the reason the woman was distraught. She'd say to the women who leaned on her for advice, for example, "What about that guy, Mark? Didn't you say he liked you?" When the woman answered yes, but noted that Mark was married, her response would often be, "I'm not telling you to marry the guy. I'm just saying you got bills and Mark can help you with those bills. Just give him a call. Hang out with him a few times. I used to know a guy who was just like Mark. I'd let him come over while the kids were sleeping. We'd hang out for a little while and then, he'd go home to his wife. I didn't care because that man was paying all of my bills. Sometimes, us mothers have to make some uncomfortable choices so that our children can eat." This is what I call a Madam Jezebel. She prostitutes the women around her, but they don't realize they're being prostituted because Jezebel is not making any money from their sexual escapades. She's just training them to become Jezebels themselves. She's taking the training wheels off their immorality, teaching them to throw all caution to the wind and encouraging them to use their bodies to get what they want.

Of course, I refused to deal with the Madam Jezebel types because even when I was in the world, I saw them for what they were: female pimps. Eventually, God saved me and as He began to grow me up, He identified the many spirits I'd came in contact with while in the world and that one, in particular, was Jezebel herself.

Jezebel: The Thief

During her reign as queen of Israel, Jezebel did much evil. It goes without saying that the person who wrote the book of Kings (believed to be Prophet Jeremiah) could not list all of the wicked things that Jezebel did during her tenure as queen. Nevertheless, to demonstrate how wicked Jezebel was, he detailed the story of Naboth's vineyard.

1 Kings 21:1-16 (ESV): *Now Naboth the Jezreelite had a vineyard in Jezreel, beside the palace of Ahab king of Samaria. And after this Ahab said to Naboth, "Give me your vineyard, that I may have it for a vegetable garden, because it is near my house, and I will give you a better vineyard for it; or, if it seems good to you, I will give you its value in money." But Naboth said to Ahab, "The Lord forbid that I should give you the inheritance of my fathers." And Ahab went into his house vexed and sullen because of what Naboth the Jezreelite had said to him, for he had said, "I will not give you the inheritance of my fathers." And he lay down on his bed and turned away his* *face and would eat no food.*

But Jezebel his wife came to him and said to him, "Why is your spirit so vexed that you eat no food?" And he said to her, "Because I spoke to Naboth the Jezreelite and said to him, 'Give me your vineyard for money, or else, if it please you, I will give you another vineyard for it.' And he answered, 'I will not give you my vineyard.'" And Jezebel his wife said to him, "Do you now govern Israel? Arise and eat bread and let your heart be cheerful; I will give you the vineyard of Naboth the Jezreelite."

So she wrote letters in Ahab's name and sealed them with his seal, and she sent the letters to the elders and the leaders who lived with Naboth in his city. And she wrote in the letters, "Proclaim a fast, and set Naboth at the head of the people. And set two worthless men opposite him, and let them bring a charge against him, saying, 'You have cursed God and the king.' Then take him out and stone him to death." And the men of his city, the elders and the leaders who lived in his city, did as Jezebel had sent word to them. As it was written in the letters that she had sent to them, they proclaimed a fast and set Naboth at the head of the people. And the two worthless men came in and sat opposite him. And the worthless men brought a charge against Naboth in the presence of the people, saying, "Naboth cursed God and the king." So they took him outside the city and stoned him to death with stones. Then they sent to Jezebel, saying, "Naboth has been stoned; he is dead."

As soon as Jezebel heard that Naboth had been stoned and was dead, Jezebel said to Ahab, "Arise, take possession of the vineyard of Naboth the Jezreelite, which he refused to give you for money, for Naboth is not alive, but dead." And as soon as Ahab heard that Naboth was dead, Ahab arose to go down to the vineyard of Naboth the Jezreelite, to take possession of it.

Ahab was king. He could have had just about any piece of land he wanted, but he had his eyes fasted on Naboth's vineyard. Instead of just accepting Naboth's rejection of his offer, Ahab decided to turn to his wicked wife. This was customary for Ahab. Some would argue that Ahab didn't know that Jezebel was going to have Naboth killed, but in truth, he did know ... or he *at least* suspected that she would. He chose to look the other way, remain ignorant of what Jezebel was planning and just wait for Jezebel's promise to give him Naboth's vineyard to come to fruition. Where is the evidence that Ahab was aware of his wife's wicked plans? It's in 1 Kings 1:17-24, where Ahab was confronted by the Prophet Elijah for his role in Naboth's death.

1 Kings 1:17-24 (ESV): *Then the word of the Lord came to Elijah the Tishbite, saying, "Arise, go down to meet Ahab king of Israel, who is in Samaria; behold, he is in the vineyard of Naboth, where he has gone to take possession.*

And you shall say to him, 'Thus says the Lord, "Have you killed and also taken possession?"' And you shall say to him, 'Thus says the Lord: "In the place where dogs licked up the blood of Naboth shall dogs lick your own blood."'"
Ahab said to Elijah, "Have you found me, O my enemy?" He answered, "I have found you, because you have sold yourself to do what is evil in the sight of the Lord. Behold, I will bring disaster upon you. I will utterly burn you up, and will cut off from Ahab every male, bond or free, in Israel. And I will make your house like the house of Jeroboam the son of Nebat, and like the house of Baasha the son of Ahijah, for the anger to which you have provoked me, and because you have made Israel to sin. And of Jezebel the Lord also said, 'The dogs shall eat Jezebel within the walls of Jezreel.' Anyone belonging to Ahab who dies in the city the dogs shall eat, and anyone of his who dies in the open country the birds of the heavens shall eat."

Notice where God blamed Ahab for Naboth's death. He told Elijah to say, "Thus says the Lord, "Have *you* killed and also taken possession?" Ahab was guilty of the sin of omission. What is a sin of omission? It's the failure to do something that the Word of God has instructed you to do. Google defines the term "sin of omission" as: *a sinful failure to perform an action.* It's more like a passive sin, whereas, a sin of commission is an active sin.

Ahab neglected to stop his wife from killing Naboth, even though she'd told him that she would get Naboth's vineyard for him and Ahab likely knew about the letters she'd sent out in his name. Nevertheless, Ahab chose to look the other way and try not to get his hands dirty with Naboth's blood. He thought that the guilt of Naboth's death would fall on someone else. Nevertheless, God declared that not only was Jezebel guilty of Naboth's death, Ahab was also to blame for Naboth's death. He was a co-conspirator and a murderer.

One of the lessons you'll learn about Jezebel is that it is a thieving spirit, but not all Jezebels are hands-on with their thievery. All too often, a person with a Jezebel spirit will send others out to do their dirty work. The truth is ... most Jezebels try to keep their own hands clean; that way, should someone need to be punished for the crimes incited by Jezebel, she can redirect the blame to the people who carried out her wicked schemes. Jezebels will oftentimes directly or indirectly incite others to steal for them.

Ask any Christian graphic designer about the types of customers they've gotten and the majority of them will tell you that some of the worst Jezebels they've had to work with hid behind the cloth. Now, don't get me wrong ... not all leaders are Jezebels. Most of them are

God-fearing and moral, but one out of every ten leaders I work with has a Jezebel spirit or jezebellic tendencies. Of course, one of my areas of trade is graphic design and I work exclusively with ministries. It goes without saying, I've seen my fair share of thefts and theft attempts. I've been criticized, ridiculed and demonized by leaders who got upset because I wouldn't do free work for their ministries, but one thing I've learned is that anywhere money is involved, there will be thieves. And not all thieves want something freely. Many of them will try to get graphic designers to severely cut their costs or operate outside of their posted rules. I remember when the Lord gave me rules to establish within my business. At first, I didn't want to post the rules or take my prices up, but the truth was ... I was getting some of the worst customers known to man and they are people who want slave labor for pennies on the dollar. At first, I was far too nice because I kept operating under a set of self-imposed rules. I had been given a unique opportunity to work with God's elect and I didn't want to abuse it or mishandle any one of the leaders that God sent my way. The problem was ... not every leader was released to be a leader, nor were they sent to me by God. My low prices and lack of rules made me an open target for the Jezebel spirit.

In the beginning, I didn't require full payment upfront

and in some cases, no payment at all. I've dealt with controlling, narcissistic leaders who were so addicted to delegating that they would not release me, despite me being finished with their designs. The design work would *never* be enough. They would request endless revisions and do-overs for the sake of having power over another human being ... or at least, the perception of power. I had to finally stop the charade in order to get out of their grips. Any graphic designer will tell you that if you do not stop this type of customer, you will end up becoming their unofficial secretary, working primarily for them with no additional pay outside of, for example, the $50 they paid you to design a flyer for them. I had to learn to do what I did not want to do in the beginning and that was ... offend some of the people in the pulpit. You would think that I'd learned my lesson after dealing with Nancy (the pastor who stalked me), but I still had such a reverence for titles that I would work tirelessly to ensure that all of my customers walked away happy. The problem with this is ... people need to be happy before they can walk away happy and honestly, there are some people out there who simply like to have power over other people. The Lord kept dealing with me about such souls and, in the beginning, I would not adhere to His voice, so He allowed me to endure thefts, manipulation, and just about any and everything I could endure.

Finally, I decided to listen to God, put some rules in

place, charge customers what my designs were worth and let the wrong customers fall away from me so I could make room for the right ones. Almost immediately, I started getting God-fearing leaders who did not have a wrongful relationship with their money. They didn't mind following the rules on my website, nor did they attempt to talk me down on my prices. I witnessed an amazing turnover and I've come to learn that anytime you don't know your own worth, the devil will send people to tell you what you're worth to him. Of course, I still get my fair share of Jezebels, but the majority of them won't work with me. They'll test me to see what type of designer I am and whether or not I'm easily manipulated, but I walk in the authority of Jesus Christ now, so manipulative Jezebels normally walk away and find someone else to abuse. Then again, the ones who are determined to work with me will almost always try to get me to abandon the safety of my rules. This is how I know when I'm working with Jezebel.

Jezebels will not follow the rules unless forced to do so. Instead, they will try to establish them. As a designer and entrepreneur, I've learned that you have to absolutely follow your own posted rules to the letter, otherwise, Jezebel will take more of your time in an attempt to steal from you. Remember, Jezebel is a ruling spirit and she hates rules unless she's the one who's set them.

Jezebels will try to create a soul tie with the busi-

ness owner or designer. Most of the Jezebels who come my way will oftentimes keep calling me and inquiring about information that's posted on my website in plain sight. After they get me on the phone, they'll start talking about themselves, their ministries, and trying to inquire about my personal life, business, and so on. In many cases, they don't know that I'm the business owner, so they'll employ the same technique I mentioned earlier. That is: they'll ask for my name, repeat it to me to let me know they're writing it down, tell me their names (and titles) and from there, they'll start trying to assert themselves and take authority. This is a theft attempt in 99.9% percent of the cases. First, they try to usurp the authority of the designer or the business owner and then, they try to do business the way they want to do business and even establish how much they want to pay. Since I recognize this technique, I tell them how to get to the page where the rules are posted (in most cases, they are already visiting the web page or have viewed it). When they challenge a rule that's posted, I kindly and professionally let them know that we don't bend our rules, nor do we exclude anyone from them. In the past, I've bent a few rules for people who claimed to not understand them and when I did this, it *always* backfired (in one hundred percent of the cases). The customer would then begin to take advantage of me, all the while, breaking other rules. The Lord had to teach me that in order for my customers to respect my rules, I needed to respect and honor them. When I started doing this, I found myself working with less Jezebels and more true men and women of God. **Jezebels will always place emphasis on their titles and their works.** They understand that many people fear and respect certain titles, so they try to tap into that fear in order to usurp authority. Thankfully, God delivered me from that fear, so it goes without saying that I've offended many Jezebels. Nevertheless, I've worked with thousands of truly awesome men and women of God, so it was all well worth it.

Jezebels will always try to get the business owner to believe that the power of the business owner's success lies in their hands. For example, one of the most common things I have heard Jezebels say to me is, "I know a lot of people and if this goes well between you and me, I'm gonna be sending a lot of folks your way. You're going to be a really busy woman." When I was immature in business, I fell for this a few times and it's not true. Whomever Jezebel sends your way will be just as cheap and manipulative as she is ... if not more. I've learned that they truly do work in networks.

Jezebels love to name-drop. Again, this is a theft attempt. They do this to make the entrepreneur or designer believe that they have the ability to promote the company by simply mentioning it to some celebrity they claim to be connected to. This is a common ploy of the Jezebel spirit and it is a lie. In most cases, Jezebel simply went to some man or woman of God's church, shook their hands and spoke with them a few times. After that, they began to use the leaders' names and if they happen to have a picture of themselves with the leader, they will use it as well.

Of course, there are many ways that Jezebel tries to steal from people, including outside of the marketplace arena. Nevertheless, the point here is ... Jezebels are cunning and manipulative thieves who will use prophecy, control, witchcraft and many other methods to get whatever it is that they want. Additionally, when they fail to get what they want, they almost always speak reproachfully about the people who did not fall into their snares. This is their way of saying, "If I cannot control you, I'll control how others see you."

Jezebel: The False Prophet
Revelation 2:20 (ESV): *But I have this against you, that you tolerate that woman Jezebel, who calls herself a prophetess and is teaching and seducing my servants to practice sexual immorality and to eat food sacrificed to idols.*

We are truly living in the days of tolerance, whereas,

people are now defending the devil more than ever. In an attempt to be politically correct, many people are trying to sympathize with folks who have the devil in them, instead of trying to usher them into an environment where they can receive counseling, emotional healing, and deliverance. That's because many people love their demons.

At the same time, many believers are so out of touch with God that, like Saul, they are thirsty for a word from God. Because of this, they turn to witches disguising themselves as prophets in an attempt to hear from God. Even when God sends them one warning after another, they refuse to yield to the voice of God because He's not answering the specific questions they have or He's not answering them the way they want to be answered. You see, sometimes God answers us through experience and sometimes, He answers us in the dimension where we need the most deliverance. He does this so that, after noticing that He's not answering us regarding a certain area of our lives, we will seek Him in those areas all the more and realize that we need deliverance in those areas. He doesn't always give us the answers to the tests of life. After all, the answers are already found in the Bible. We simply need to open it, study it, meditate on the Word of God and seek the heart of God through prayer and fasting. But because many believers are too lazy, too self-absorbed, and too anxious to get whatever it is that they want, they think that they can avoid the path of obedience and take an alternate route to a prophet. This almost always leads them into Jezebel's trap, where they will receive divination disguised as prophecies.

1 Samuel 28:3-14 (ESV): *Now Samuel had died, and all Israel had mourned for him and buried him in Ramah, his own city. And Saul had put the mediums and the necromancers out of the land. The Philistines assembled and came and encamped at Shunem. And Saul gathered all Israel, and they encamped at Gilboa. When Saul saw the army of the Philistines, he was afraid, and his heart trembled greatly. And when Saul inquired of the Lord, the Lord did not answer him, either by dreams, or by Urim, or by prophets. Then Saul said to his servants, "Seek out for me a woman who is a medium, that I may go to her and inquire of her." And his servants said to him, "Behold, there is a medium at En-dor."*

So Saul disguised himself and put on other garments and went, he and two men with him. And they came to the woman by night. And he said, "Divine for me by a spirit and bring up for me whomever I shall name to you." The woman said to him, "Surely you know what Saul has done, how he has cut off the mediums and the necromancers from the land. Why then are you laying a trap for my life to bring about my death?" But Saul swore to her by the Lord, "As the Lord lives, no punishment shall come upon you for this thing." Then the woman said, "Whom shall I bring up for you?" He said, "Bring up Samuel for me." When the woman saw Samuel, she cried out with a loud voice. And the woman said to Saul, "Why have you deceived me? You are Saul." The king said to her, "Do not be afraid. What do you see?" And the woman said to Saul, "I see a god coming up out of the earth." He said to her, "What is his appearance?" And she said, "An old man is coming up, and he is wrapped in a robe." And Saul knew that it was Samuel, and he bowed with his face to the ground and paid homage.

This is the very same thing many believers are doing today. They are disobedient, disloyal servants who abuse their authority to get what they want. When they don't hear from God, they look for alternate ways to get instructions, including going to false prophets in search of a word from God. When the false prophet is exposed, they are the first ones to defend him because the false prophet is the only voice they are hearing!

False prophets capitalize off God's people. They often use divination (the spirit of python) to receive psychic readings from the spirit realm. They disguise their payments as seed offerings. For example, an apostle exposed a man disguising himself as a woman and calling himself a prophetess. When I went to the man's Facebook page, he had a video up where he'd began to "prophesy," but the first thing that caught my attention on that video was an image directly over his head. It was a painting of Buddha. Any man or woman who hears from God, especially a prophet or an apostle will tell you that the Buddha symbol alone is demonic. It is a symbol of witchcraft! Most, if not all, of the true prophets and apostles I've spoken with cannot and will not own anything that represents a false deity. Most of them can't even be in a room with witchcraft symbols or witches without getting a headache or some form of tension in their bodies. For example, I purchased some throw pillows from a retail store a few months ago and almost immediately, I started getting headaches and a lot of tension in my neck. I knew that something was off, so I started praying about it. A few days after purchasing the pillows, I was at my computer working when all of a sudden, the Lord drew my attention to my couch. My eyes immediately fixated on the throw pillows. The pillows had gold-toned specks on them that initially appeared to be randomly placed, but when I looked at them that evening, I saw an image of a lotus. It was a Hindu symbol. My prayers had been answered. The source of my tension was a witchcraft symbol. Even though it was the middle of the night when I noticed the symbol, I could not let the pillows stay in my house for another second. I immediately took them outside, placed them in my car, found the receipt and put it away. The headache lifted the very minute I got those pillows out of my house! I stayed awake until the next morning and took the pillows back to the store I'd purchased them from. Understand this: true prophets understand that the spirit realm is nothing to be lackadaisical about. You cannot use the "God knows my heart" defense when dealing with the prophetic. The point is ... false prophets do see visions and hear voices! I'm not saying that everyone who's seen demonic visions or heard demonic voices are false prophets. They very well may be true prophets in need of deliverance. What I am saying, however, is that you cannot believe every spirit that speaks to you or appears before you, including the ones that manifest in folks boasting of religious titles. You have to test the spirits!

1 John 4:1 (ESV): *Beloved, do not believe every spirit, but test the spirits to see whether they are from God, for many false prophets have gone out into the world.*

God has assigned me to the ministry of deliverance and every time I have a conference call where I start calling out spirits, one of the networks that God has me calling out is spirits that came in through false prophecy. It was and always is disheartening to hear the number of people on the line who begin to cough, yawn and vomit ... these are people who are going through deliverance from spirits that entered their lives through their encounters with false prophets.

Being lazy with God will almost always lead to an encounter with Jezebel. I've learned that any access to the realm of the spirit without having an intimate relationship with God can be dangerous. It is your relationship with the Lord that will help you to understand whose voice you are hearing.

John 10:4-5 (ESV): *When he has brought out all his own, he goes before them, and the sheep follow him, for they know his voice. A stranger they will not follow, but they will flee from him, for they do not know the voice of strangers."*

Jezebel: The Boss
Most people can testify about having at least one manager or supervisor who was bound by the Jezebel spirit. When Jezebel is your boss, she will make your job a living hell ... especially if you're not one of her favorite people.

Jezebellic bosses love the power they have over others. They love knowing that the power to keep or terminate a person lies within their hands. They love knowing that they can dominate and control people without being challenged. For this reason, people who have the Jezebel spirit tend to be highly ambitious. Wherever they are, they will work tirelessly to ascend the ranks of authority. They are oftentimes very hard workers who are loyal to their crafts, plus, they are often punctual and dependable. Nevertheless, their evil is more evident to the people who are under their authority and not-so-much to the people who outrank them. They will backbite, lie and cheat their way to the top.

When I was around 17 or 18 years old, I worked in retail as a cashier. I was one of those cashiers who wanted to capture the attention of my superiors in a positive way, but truthfully, I wasn't looking for promotion (even though I wouldn't have turned it down either). I wanted to be favored and I definitely wanted a raise, so I followed the rules and tried to excel in everything I did.

One day, a group of ladies stood in my line. I don't remember if there were two or three women, but what I do remember is that the women were behaving suspiciously. Something about them told me that I needed to pay special attention when ringing them up. When their turn came, they loaded a few items onto the conveyor belt before loading a comforter onto the conveyor belt. The cashiers at the store I worked for had been trained to open any and everything that could be easily opened by customers, including comforters. If we found anything in, for example, containers, shoe boxes or comforters, we weren't allowed to accuse the customer of theft or attempted theft. Instead, our job was to pull those items out and start scanning them.

Sure enough, when I unzipped the comforter, there were all sorts of items stashed away between the folds, with most of it being electronic stuff. Inwardly, I was excited because I'd busted a thief ... even though I couldn't say anything to them and they couldn't be legally arrested. When one of my supervisors walked by, she noticed me pulling the items out of the comforter and scanning them. She stood behind me and watched and, of course, I was overly excited because I thought she'd tell the managers how good of a job I'd done and I'd get a raise or a bonus. The customers stopped me, claiming they didn't know how those items had gotten into the comforter and asked me to remove them from their ticket and I did. They ended up purchasing the comforter because they didn't want to look guilty and they left. After they walked away, the supervisor walked away and I was sure she was going to share the news with my manager. A few minutes later, I got called into the manager's office. I shut my line down and rushed to the office in excitement. I'd followed the rules they'd set and stopped a theft.

I walked into the manager's office with a big smile on

my face, but I noticed that my manager wasn't smiling; plus, the supervisor was sitting in the room as well and she wasn't smiling. She couldn't even look at me. To my surprise, the supervisor had lied to the manager and told him that I didn't follow protocol. She claimed that she was walking by and noticed that I didn't check the comforter, so she told me to check it. According to her, when I did go back and check the comforter, that's when I found all of the items. She took full credit for what I'd done. *I was devastated.* She even had the audacity to try to advise me while I sat there with tears in my eyes trying to defend myself. Of course, I was young and in the world then, but I had such a positive view of people in authority.

What the supervisor had done was a classic Jezebel move. Jezebel likes to take credit for the good things that others do, all the while, avoiding blame for all the bad things that they themselves do. I didn't know anything about demons back then, but when I look back over my life, I can now identify the many encounters I had with Jezebel in the workplace and that was one of them. I walked out of the manager's office more angry than I was brokenhearted. I didn't realize it then, but the enemy was training me to become a Jezebel by allowing me to be hurt, mishandled and lied on by authority figures. That's because I had such a respect for people in authority and this made it difficult for Satan to use me at the level he wanted to use me at.

Another encounter I had with Jezebel took place at that same store when I was a young cashier. Another one of the supervisors was an older woman who simply did not like me or my closest friend (she was also a cashier). Neither of us understood why the woman didn't like us, nevertheless, we went out of our way to excel at doing our jobs, and we tried hard to impress our leaders. One of the things I noticed about that particular supervisor was that she loved the women who were like herself ... women who liked to stand around and gossip. Even though I was in the world then, gossip wasn't my forte.

My friend and I noticed that the supervisor kept putting us on the cash registers that we (the cashiers) referred to as "death row." Death row consisted of about six registers that more than 80 percent of the customers came to. They would always be the busiest registers. Normally, the supervisors were supposed to rotate the cashiers so, for example, if a cashier worked on "death row" the previous day, she was supposed to be placed on one of the slower registers the next day. This was to make things fair and ensure that all cashiers would have an equal amount of busy and not-so-busy days. Nevertheless, the supervisor would place her favorite cashiers (her gossiping buddies) on the slow registers and place Sharon and I on "death row" every time we were scheduled. Nevertheless, we didn't utter a complaint about what she was doing, even though we knew that her treatment of us was unfair. At the same time, the supervisor would always speak harshly to us, and when we worked on the slow registers, she would always ensure that we had something to do.

There was another cashier who noticed how the supervisor treated Sharon and I and it was her (we'll call her Angelic) who, to our surprise, went and complained about the supervisor to one of the managers. Ironically enough, even though she wasn't a gossiper, Angelic happened to be one of the cashiers that the supervisor favored. *I believe this was because of how outspoken she was.* Angelic knew that Sharon and I were young girls who were too afraid of losing our jobs to speak up, so she spoke up on our behalf. At the same time, we didn't personally know Angelic outside of greeting her anytime we saw her, so when a manager stopped and asked us about the supervisors' treatment of us, we reluctantly told her the truth. She asked if it were true that the supervisor placed Sharon and I on "death row" every time we were scheduled and we told her yes. A few days later, we saw the supervisor wearing a blue smock, meaning, she had been demoted.

Everywhere that there is a Jezebel and an Ahab, there is also a defender of God's people named Jehoshaphat. Angelic was our Jehoshaphat and ironically enough, the manager who demoted the supervisor was one of the key instruments God eventually used to lead me to salvation.

When Jezebel is your boss, she will use your fear of being terminated or demoted to control you. She will also use her influence to control how others perceive you. Nowadays, as a leader, I receive many emails from people complaining about wicked, controlling bosses who appear to be overly determined to either get them terminated, cause them to quit or make their jobs a living hell. Unfortunately, when dealing with a jezebellic boss, the only thing you can do is pray, follow the rules and if at all possible, go through some training programs so you can become Jezebel's equal or her boss. That's the only way to confront Jezebel, otherwise, a Jehu has to arise to confront her.

I've found that almost everywhere you go, you are going to find a person bound and influenced by the Jezebel spirit, but this doesn't mean that they will always be your leader. Sometimes, all it takes is a simple prayer from a broken and contrite spirit to provoke God to move on your behalf. A good example of this happened when I was married to Roger. He was new to a company and he'd worked there a few months when they placed him under a woman who we'll call "Betty." Betty definitely had a Jezebel spirit. She was drunk with power and she made Roger's job difficult.

One day, Roger came home from work frustrated and when I asked him what was wrong, he started telling me about Betty. She would give him an assignment to do and then, switch his assignment before he completed it. A few hours later or the next day, she'd switch him up again ... even though he'd tell her that he wasn't finished with the initial assignment. At this, she would respond that the new assignment was more important. A few hours later or the next day, she'd ask him why he hadn't completed the former assignments. When he would remind her that she'd stopped him and placed him in another area, she would berate him. He was an overachiever and he felt that his job was on the line because of Betty's instability.

I had become somewhat of a mature believer by then, so I went before the Lord in prayer. I prayed for Roger and I began to war against the Jezebel spirit operating at his workplace. God surely answered the prayer and one of Roger's managers came to him and said that he'd been watching him and noticed how good of a job he'd been doing. He also apologized for placing him under Betty and he acknowledged how poorly he noticed Betty had been treating him. That day, he placed Roger under the rank of a manager who actually favored him. The point is ... prayer works!

One of the worst things a believer can be is an under-achiever because we must always remember that Jezebel is an overachiever. If Jezebel is more determined to rise to the top than you are, you will spend many sleepless nights wondering if you'll have a job to go to in the morning.

Proverbs 29:2 (ESV): *When the righteous increase, the people rejoice, but when the wicked rule, the people groan.*

Proverbs 29:16 (ESV): *When the wicked increase, transgression increases, but the righteous will look upon their downfall.*

Jezebel: The Protective Predator

It is essential for believers to understand that not every protective soul is looking out for their best interest. Not everyone who appears to be protecting you is actually protecting you. Some people are simply guarding what they feel to be their property. This is very similar to how a dog treats a bone. When he attacks another dog for coming too close to his bone, it's not because he loves and wants to protect the bone. He does this because, to him, the bone belongs to him and he plans to devour it.

Sometimes, Jezebels can appear to be nurturing, protective and motherly (or fatherly). They will offer their prey a place to stay, food to eat and even pray for them when they're broken. This is all a ploy to gain control over the person.

One of the most common disguises Jezebel wears is that of a protector. This is because most people who have the Jezebel spirit are still hurting from wounds that they've acquired years ago. They are oftentimes vengeful souls who look for opportunities to avenge their own pain by attacking people who remind them of the people who once preyed on them. Anytime you go to Jezebel talking about another person who has wronged or hurt you, Jezebel does not see an opportunity to defend you, even though her words and her actions will appear otherwise. Jezebel sees an opportunity to feel justified in doing evil to another person. You are nothing but another soul who gave Jezebel an opportunity to perform her witchcraft. A good example of this is some of the ministries tailored towards hurting women. Now, let me say this ... not all ministries targeting hurting women are ran by Jezebels or have an ungodly agenda, but many of them are. Jezebels are often created in pain, so a place where hurting women run to looking for help is the perfect recruiting center and training grounds for Jezebels to raise up new Jezebels.

Jezebels will always want to know the full stories behind your pain or anger. This is why forgiveness is so very important to the believer. They will want the names of the people who've hurt you and they'll want as much detailed information as they can get regarding your offenders. They will pray with you and pray for you before preying on you. If they see that your pain has blinded you or that anger has hijacked your discernment, they'll even start speaking death over the person or people who've hurt you. I've seen this several times. This is the reason I tell people to get in the safety of good, godly counselors while they are at peace; that way, they won't allow their emotions to drive them into a witchcraft establishment whenever they find themselves in one of life's trials. The truth is ... when you're hurting, anyone who is defending you or appears to be defending you will look like a righteous hero when they may very well be the opposite.

If you watch a lot of criminal investigative shows, you'll see stories about women, for example, who've taken in broken and hurting teenagers. They'll take on the motherly role when those children don't have loving protective mothers. They will feed them, give them a place to stay and let them do whatever they want to do under their roofs. Nevertheless, once offended, Jezebel will send the children out to do wicked things like scaring, attacking or even taking the lives of the people they were offended with. Of course, when caught, the women would redirect the blame to the children who'd carried out their evil instructions, but after realizing they'd been preyed upon, the children would slowly begin to tell the truth. Jezebels love to create what can best be described as "tool sheds" where the people they want to use as tools can congregate and be used by them.

Jezebels will fight for you, go to court on your behalf and even side with you when you're wrong, but make no mistake about it, Jezebel is only defending her plate and the people on it.

The truth is ... Jezebel has many faces, and all of them couldn't be listed in one book. However, one of the quickest ways to discern the Jezebel spirit is to simply pray, don't be so quick to talk, and always listen enough so you can test the spirit in the person who's speaking. Jezebels are overly obsessed with power and anytime you come across a person who is trying to usurp the power of another human being, you have come across Jezebel!

CHAPTER 8

The Great Jezebellion

The Jezebel spirit is not a simple demon who comes to terrorize an individual. Its goal is far more advanced than simply perverting a young girl through rape. Satan thinks in numbers; he thinks in generations, territories and governments, so his agenda (through Jezebel) is to use that girl to capture men through soul ties and to birth children who have no covering (head of home, father). The head of the wife, as instituted by God, is the husband and contrary to popular belief, a man does not become a woman's husband at the altar. Marriage is established in God's eyes through sex, but it is the order in which sex takes place that determines if the sex is legal or illegal (fornication). Because Jezebel is a ruler and a principality, its goal is to remove the covering of the woman; that way, it can control her and it can control the children that are birthed through her. It then moves horizontally through her children, using them to help spread its agenda through peer association, peer pressure and when they get old enough, through sex.

Of course, if the woman truly repents of her fornication and submits herself fully to God, she can rid her outer courts of every demonic spirit that once called it home. Some spirits are more stubborn so she may require extensive Christian counseling to get and keep them out. **James 4:7 (ESV):** *Submit yourselves therefore to God. Resist the devil, and he will flee from you.*

Of course, a man can have the Jezebel spirit as well because demons do not possess genders, nor are they prejudiced. The Jezebel spirit works more effectively in women and that's why it prefers to enter women over men, but it will enter men if doing so serves Jezebel's agenda. For example, if the Jezebel spirit wants access to a woman's life, but she is resistant to it, it will attempt to enter her life through associations. Those associations include jezebellic friends, leaders, family members or men bound by the Jezebel spirit. It will also attempt to enter her life through music and any form of media she allows to enter her ear-gates or eye-gates. For this reason, we often hear people saying things like, "Why do I keep meeting the same kind of men?" or "Why do I keep meeting the same type of women?" The truth is ... Jezebel is a strategic spirit that will stop at nothing to accomplish its agenda.

If Jezebel wants to operate through a man, it will use

him to usurp power from his wife, his children and anyone he has any form of authority over. This makes no sense to the carnal mind, given that God has already given a man authority over his wife, but in truth, there is a such thing as *legal* authority (power given and authorized by God) versus *illegal* authority (illegal or excessive use of power). A man having legal authority is a man who is submitted to God and leads his family in Christ Jesus. A man tapping into illegal authority will be self-absorbed, selfishly ambitious and not submitted to God. He will use his God-given authority, fear, manipulation, physical strength and his intimate access to his wife to control her. This is illegal and demonic. Just because a man has authority over his wife does not mean he possesses *absolute* power over her. She still has the ability to choose to do right or wrong. She still has the freedom of will. Both people are required by God to come together under the umbrella of obedience. If a man abuses his authority, it then becomes an illegal use of power. For example, police officers have authority, but they do not have *absolute* power over the people they are confronting or arresting. If they abuse their authority, they have perverted their power and as such, their behaviors can be judged as illegal.

A good example of Jezebel operating through a man is when a man is physically and emotionally abusive towards his wife. Another good example is when Jezebel enters an unmarried man and uses him, through promiscuity, to uncover unmarried women. This means that the man in question is uncovered, and therefore, is a weapon formed against the women he is sent to seduce or uncover. It goes without saying that when this happens, Jezebel will employ seducing spirits through that man to manipulate and seduce women. Once he accomplishes his agenda, the demons that influence his habits and beliefs will change the way he sees each woman, thus, causing him to become bored with them or disgusted by them. After this happens, the man walks away, leaving the woman uncovered, feeling rejected and open for demonic attack and persuasion. Again, the Jezebel spirit thinks in numbers and its goal is to move horizontally so that it can move vertically.

If a believer goes through deliverance but does not allow the Holy Spirit to come in and fill the places that were emptied out or purged, the spirits that were cast out will come back with seven spirits more wicked than themselves. The reason for this is ... the courts that were once cleansed have become a womb where new beliefs have been born or are currently developing. Filling those courts would mean that the enemy will now have to compete with the new information and will be easily detected, so he no longer wants to move horizontally; he needs to advance in the believer's subconscious. He also wants to send in higher-ranking spirits that the deliverance minister may not be familiar with. The reason for this is ... some spirits won't come out just by the deliverance minister shouting, "Come out of him!" Instead, some require fasting *and* prayer to be removed (Mark 9:29).

The subconscious has several levels, with each one providing a foundation for the next level. Again, the enemy's goal is to get closest to the unconscious mind, therefore, if allowed back into a person who's been delivered, the enemy needs to use higher-ranking spirits. He needs to use demons that can initially access levels of the believer's mind that the former spirits could not access. Such spirits don't have to work their way "up" They simply step in on the levels that mirror their ranks. Those spirits also mirror the level of rebellion the believer has submitted himself or herself to.

Jezebel in Government

In the United States of America, we have seen a huge influx of demonic powers. It may all appear to be sudden, but in truth, the enemy has been moving upon this nation for a long time. Nowadays, Jezebel has effectively removed prayer from schools and has been tirelessly working to remove the "in God we trust" insignia from our money.

What made the United States government so easy to attack was the fact that we are a tolerable nation, whereas, God tells us in the book of Revelations 2:20 to not tolerate Jezebel. Our government boasts on being "of the people, by the people and for the people." This was part of the Gettysburg Address, a speech that Abraham Lincoln gave during the American Civil War. Below is a part of that speech:

"But, in a larger sense, we can not dedicate—we can not consecrate—we can not hallow—this ground. The brave men, living and dead, who struggled here, have consecrated it, far above our poor power to add or detract. The world will little note, nor long remember what we say here, but it can never forget what they did here. It is for us the living, rather, to be dedicated here to the unfinished work which they who fought here have thus far so nobly advanced. It is rather for us to be here dedicated to the great task remaining before us—that from these honored dead we take increased devotion to that cause for which they gave the last full measure of devotion—that we here highly resolve that these dead shall not have died in vain—that this nation, under God, shall have a new birth of freedom—and that government of the people, by the people, for the people, shall not perish from the earth" (Abraham Lincoln).

Today, Americans love to quote the "of the people, by the people and for the people" portion, but somehow seem to overlook the part that reads, "this nation, **under God**, shall have a new birth of freedom." These words were not only powerful enough to be recorded and used by America as a motto of sorts, but they were also prophetic. If we, as a nation, would only stay under God, we would have and maintain our freedom. Sadly enough, the Jezebel spirit has started a revolution in this country and its goal is to remove YAHWEH. So, this nation is slowly becoming *"of the people, by the people and for the people"* but the people don't have a godly covering because they don't want to be "under God." This means that we are slowly losing our freedom, but darkness has blinded us to this fact.

Proverbs 4:19 (ESV): *The way of the wicked is like deep darkness; they do not know over what they stumble.*

2 Chronicles 7:13-14 (ESV): *When I shut up the heavens so that there is no rain, or command the locust to devour the land, or send pestilence among my people, if my people who are called by my name humble themselves, and pray and seek my face and turn from their wicked ways, then I will hear from heaven and will forgive their sin and heal their land.*

There are no battles, laws or attacks against any other religious establishments such as there are against the

Christian faith in these days. Atheists and Agnostics have arisen and declared war against Christianity. Christians are being persecuted for not complying with New Age beliefs and for not submitting to the beliefs of others. We're the only people who can be sued for saying the name of our God in certain arenas, even though other religions can say their god's or gods' names without consequence. The Jezebel spirit has bewitched this nation and at first, we saw this in the media and then the government. Now, we are seeing Jezebel take over homes and churches. We've witnessed such an outcry of people demanding the right to sin against God, all the while, attempting to muzzle Christians. This is the demon or principality we refer to as Jezebel and it is taking over this nation right before our eyes.

Jezebel, the woman, gave Ahab what he wanted in exchange for his authority. This is the same thing that's going on in our governmental offices today. Wicked and wealthy people run this nation and they fund our governmental leaders' campaigns in exchange for the leaders' authority. This means that many of our leaders are nothing but Jezebel puppets whose masters are the people who pay for their advertisements. At the same time, lower-ranking Jezebel spirits have moved through families, creating a wave of hurt, poverty and a demand for power and control. Anytime a leader is ungodly, the people will become ungodly, and sadly enough, this nation is run by ungodly leaders. Remember, before Ahab became king of Israel, the Israelites worshiped YAHWEH, but once he became king, Jezebel turned his heart to Baal. He then turned the people of God's heart to Baal. This is the same thing we are witnessing today.

Proverbs 29:2 (ESV): *When the righteous increase, the people rejoice, but when the wicked rule, the people groan.*

Jezebel in Media

If you turn on your television, you will be inundated with sexually suggestive media. In this day and age, raw talent is not a requirement to stand in front of a camera or hold a mic. The media is looking for anything sexy or controversial. This is Jezebel's witchcraft in full effect.

Many of this world's celebrities today have boasted about selling their souls to the devil, performing witchcraft or being demonically possessed. They promote sex, violence and the love of money ... all of which are under the Baal principality. People are now "idolizing" people ... and tithing into the unseen governments in which each celebrity promotes.

Romans 1:18-27 (ESV): *For the wrath of God is revealed from heaven against all ungodliness and unrighteousness of men, who by their unrighteousness suppress* *the truth. For what can be known about God is plain to them, because God has shown it to them. For his invisible attributes, namely, his eternal power and divine nature, have been clearly perceived, ever since the creation of the world, in the things that have been made. So they are without excuse. For although they knew God, they did not honor him as God or give thanks to him, but they became futile in their thinking, and their foolish hearts were darkened. Claiming to be wise, they became fools, and exchanged the glory of the immortal God for images resembling mortal man and birds and animals and creeping things. Therefore God gave them up in the lusts of their hearts to impurity, to the dishonoring of their bodies among themselves, because they exchanged the truth about God for a lie and worshiped and served the creature rather than the Creator, who is blessed forever! Amen.*

For this reason God gave them up to dishonorable passions. For their women exchanged natural relations for those that are contrary to nature; and the men likewise gave up natural relations with women and were consumed with passion for one another, men committing shameless acts with men and receiving in themselves the due penalty for their error.

This nation is now bewitched and many of the people in it are moving like demonic spirits. They've successfully removed prayer from school, God from government and now, they are moving into the inner courts and that is ... the church!

Galatians 3:1 (ESV): *O foolish Galatians, who hath bewitched you, that ye should not obey the truth, before whose eyes Jesus Christ hath been evidently set forth, crucified among you?*

Mark 13:14 (ESV): *But when you see the abomination of desolation standing where he ought not to be (let the reader understand), then let those who are in Judea flee to the mountains.*

Please understand how this works. If the enemy could control the church (which he cannot), he would control the part of this government that is responsible for our strength and success. It is the part of the government that breathes, even though there is darkness all around it. His strategies include, but are not limited to:

1. Placing false teachers in the pulpits.
2. Sending ungodly believers out to witness.
3. Disguising ungodly organizations as Christian organizations.
4. Causing believers to be double-minded and unstable.
5. Searing the conscious of believers so that they won't know the truth from a lie.
6. Redefining the word love to mean "inclusion." *In-*

clusion is just another word for tolerance.
7. Creating and establishing laws that prevent the name of Jesus from being spoken.
8. Creating and establishing laws that rid Christians of their rights, thus, making us secondary citizens or *unofficial* slaves.
9. Bringing occult practices into the church.
10. Ahab'ing the church.

Placing false teachers in the pulpits: By placing false teachers in the pulpits, Satan can turn many believers away from church and ultimately, away from God. This is why we have now coined the term "church hurt." This also discourages unbelievers from getting saved, all the while, justifying attacks against the church from ungodly organizations. Additionally, it causes a traumatic distrust for leadership, thus, encouraging the "fight or flight" response that we have come to refer to as "church-hopping." The goal of the "false teacher" spirit is to turn people's hearts away from Christ Jesus or turn them against Him. To turn "away from" Him means to not believe in Him, but to turn against Him means to war against Him, even though you believe in His existence. Remember, demons do believe in Jesus.
Matthew 7:15 (ESV): *Beware of false prophets, who come to you in sheep's clothing but inwardly are ravenous wolves.*

2 John 1:7 (ESV): *For many deceivers have gone out into the world, those who do not confess the coming of Jesus Christ in the flesh. Such a one is the deceiver and the antichrist.*
James 2:19 (ESV): *You believe that God is one; you do well. Even the demons believe—and shudder!*

Sending ungodly believers out to witness: When I was married to Roger, I asked him a simple question. *Why do some African villages attack the missionaries that come to help them?* He told me that many people come to Africa disguising themselves as missionaries, but when they get there, they are taking the wealth of the land, performing all types of scientific experiments on the people and raping the women and children. I was so appalled that I accused him of lying. As time went on, I saw more news and viral newsletters that told the stories of ungodly missionaries entering African countries and doing exactly what Roger said they were doing. Of course, not all missionaries are demonically led. Many truly go to the nation to help where help is needed, but because of the trauma inflicted by the evil ones, many African villages and nations would rather attack the good ones than to risk receiving the bad ones. This doesn't just happen in Africa, but it also happens on U.S. soil. We see a lot of people who claim to be witnesses of the faith, but are nothing but wolves in sheep's clothing.

We've watched in horror as the media brought us the news of priests molesting children, married pastors being caught in hotels with prostitutes and pastors kicking members out for not paying their tithes. Make no mistake about it ... this is a demonic attempt to assassinate the Christian faith by attempting to discredit its leaders. False leaders are setting the stage for true leaders to be attacked.

Disguising ungodly organizations as Christian organizations: A great example of an ungodly organization that hides behind the Christian label is the Ku Klux Klan. Many non-white believers have turned away from the faith because false religions and groups are rising and claiming that Christianity was nothing but the white man's attempt to control his slaves. Of course, we know that this is not true since Christianity was around and thriving before slavery. However, since organizations like the Ku Klux Klan hide their hatred behind Christian labels, other ungodly associations have used this fact to drive many non-white believers away from the faith. There are many organizations rising up and asking Christians, "Did God really say that?" or "Are you serving the right god?" They plant seeds of doubt into the believer in an attempt to infiltrate and contaminate the believer's belief system and ultimately, remove the light out of the believer. That way, demons can reside in and use the now former or re*formed* believer.

Isaiah 29:13-14 (ESV): *And the Lord said: "Because this people draw near with their mouth and honor me with their lips, while their hearts are far from me, and their fear of me is a commandment taught by men, therefore, behold, I will again do wonderful things with this people, with wonder upon wonder; and the wisdom of their wise men shall perish, and the discernment of their discerning men shall be hidden."*

Causing believers to be double-minded and unstable: Double-mindedness is caused by double indoctrination or attempting to filter the truth through fact-filters. This means that a person first establishes facts as truth and then, attempts to make sense out of the truth using the facts he or she has been taught. The enemy has successfully created ungodly religions that don't wear religious tags, don't have religious buildings, and don't teach from religious books. What are these organizations? They are the people we call "celebrities" (the ungodly ones, of course). Each celebrity represents a belief, a mindset and a doctrine. By celebrating and funding the celebrity, each person knowingly or unknowingly helps that person to gain more followers, more power and more recognition. Ironically enough, many "church dollars" are being used to fund jezebellic celebrities who are nothing but the equivalent of demon costumes.

When believers follow ungodly celebrities, they become desensitized to sin and double-minded. They also become Satan's most effective weapon *against* the church. When leaders, for example, speak a controversial truth, it is the double-minded believers who "expose" them and cry out against them the loudest. Understand this: the most effective warfare takes place when spies are involved.

James 1:5-8 (ESV): *If any of you lacks wisdom, let him ask God, who gives generously to all without reproach, and it will be given him. But let him ask in faith, with no doubting, for the one who doubts is like a wave of the sea that is driven and tossed by the wind. For that person must not suppose that he will receive anything from the Lord; he is a double-minded man, unstable in all his ways.*

James 4:4 (ESV): *You adulterous people! Do you not know that friendship with the world is enmity with God? Therefore whoever wishes to be a friend of the world makes himself an enemy of God.*

Searing the conscious of believers so that they won't know the truth from a lie: Many believers today are so confused that they study with various religions in an attempt to find the truth. At the same time, many *compromised* believers have become so desensitized to sin that they are demanding that sin be allowed in church and on the stages in the church. However, because their consciences have been seared or dried out, they can't seem to hear anyone who tells them what the *uncompromising* Word of God says. When this happens, the believer becomes spiritually deaf (in a sense) and will no longer respond to words; they have to witness (or see) the power of God in action before their ears will open to allow the truth in. Such people are bewitched and under the spell of Jezebel.

Galatians 3:1 (KJV): *O foolish Galatians, who hath bewitched you, that ye should not obey the truth, before whose eyes Jesus Christ hath been evidently set forth, crucified among you?*

1 Corinthians 5:6 (ESV): *Your boasting is not good. Do you not know that a little leaven leavens the whole lump?*

Redefining the word love to mean "inclusion": The truth, even when told in love, is now being referred to as "hate speech" when it does not coincide with man's lustful desires. When people don't want to change, they try to change the Word of God. In this day and hour, the world has successfully ahab'ed many churches and is now telling leaders how to lead and believers what to believe. A great example of this is homosexuality. We know what the Word of God says regarding homosexuality; it's clearly printed in the Bible. However, pastors are now being bullied by the Jezebel spirit and told to not preach against it. This means that the world is attempting to edit the Holy Bible itself! We are undoubtedly living in the end times and no one can deny this ... not even the pagans! Foxnews.com reported the following on October 14, 2014: *The city of Houston has issued subpoenas demanding a group of pastors turn over any sermons dealing with homosexuality, gender identity or Annise Parker, the city's first openly lesbian mayor. And those ministers who fail to comply could be held in contempt of court.* Thankfully, the petition was eventually thrown out, but this goes to show the direction in which Jezebel is heading. We cannot accept what God has rejected, otherwise, we pit ourselves against a God who cannot and will not lose!

Leviticus 18:22 (ESV): *You shall not lie with a male as with a woman; it is an abomination.*

1 Corinthians 6:9-11 (ESV): *Or do you not know that the unrighteous will not inherit the kingdom of God? Do not be deceived: neither the sexually immoral, nor idolaters, nor adulterers, nor men who practice homosexuality, nor thieves, nor the greedy, nor drunkards, nor revilers, nor swindlers will inherit the kingdom of God. And such were some of you. But you were washed, you were sanctified, you were justified in the name of the Lord Jesus Christ and by the Spirit of our God.*

Proverbs 1:10-18 (ESV): *My son, if sinners entice you, do not consent. If they say, "Come with us, let us lie in wait for blood; let us ambush the innocent without reason; like*

Sheol let us swallow them alive, and whole, like those who go down to the pit; we shall find all precious goods, we shall fill our houses with plunder; throw in your lot among us; we will all have one purse"—my son, do not walk in the way with them; hold back your foot from their paths, for their feet run to evil, and they make haste to shed blood. For in vain is a net spread in the sight of any bird, but these men lie in wait for their own blood; they set an ambush for their own lives.

Creating and establishing laws that prevent the name of Jesus from being spoken: In April of 2016, Foxnews.com reported the following: *A permit is required before students can talk about Jesus at North Carolina State University, according to a lawsuit filed in federal court.* This is the first of many laws and guidelines being established to keep the name of Jesus from being spoken in governmental establishments and some public places. This includes schools. What's ironic is ... in many of these places, it is not a crime or an offense to use the Lord's name in an expletive way, but to speak of Him as your Lord can be severely punished.

Acts 4:13-21 (ESV): *Now when they saw the boldness of Peter and John, and perceived that they were uneducated, common men, they were astonished. And they recognized that they had been with Jesus. But seeing the man who was healed standing beside them, they had nothing to say* *in opposition. But when they had commanded them to leave the council, they conferred with one another, saying, "What shall we do with these men? For that a notable sign has been performed through them is evident to all the inhabitants of Jerusalem, and we cannot deny it. But in order that it may spread no further among the people, let us warn them to speak no more to anyone in this name." So they called them and charged them not to speak or teach at all in the name of Jesus. But Peter and John answered them, "Whether it is right in the sight of God to listen to you rather than to God, you must judge, for we cannot but speak of what we have seen and heard." And when they had further threatened them, they let them go, finding no way to punish them, because of the people, for all were praising God for what had happened.*

Creating and establishing laws that rid Christians of their rights, thus, making them *secondary citizens* or *unofficial slaves*: Many laws are being created to silence and spiritually castrate Christians. Why is this? There is power in our words and the enemy knows this. Jezebel wants to make eunuchs out of Christian believers! Why is this? Eunuchs have no ability to reproduce. By silencing Christians, the enemy is trying to take away our ability to reproduce other believers through evangelism. The enemy is attempting to make Christianity dormant and he wants Christians to be an endangered species. He can't remove Christ, so he wants to control Christians. At the same time, silent living people are called *slaves*. Slaves have no right to speak unless granted this permission by the slave's owner. Jezebel is attempting, in this hour, to take believers back to Egypt to become slaves of an ungodly people. In other words, God has given us (believers) dominion and authority over devils, but devils are trying to take dominion and authority over us! This is the reason that God told us to not become a part of this world. When we ally ourselves with the world who hates our God, we (in a sense) ally ourselves with and empower the very Egyptians who want to destroy us.

Bringing occult practices into the church: Yoga and karate are two examples of occultist practices that were established by Eastern (pagan) religions. Google defines "yoga" this way: *The meaning of the word "Yoga" is "union". It is derived from the Sanskrit root "yuj," (pron. "yug") meaning "to join", "to unite" but also "to subjugate", with the meaning also "to control" and "to disciplinate". The English word "yoke" is also derived from the same Sanskrit (Indo-European) root.* Yogavedics report the following information about yoga: *The beginnings of Yoga were developed by the Indus-Sarasvati civilization in Northern India over 5,000 years ago. The word yoga was first mentioned in the old-*

est sacred texts, the Rig Veda. The Vedas were a collection of texts containing songs, mantras and rituals to be used by Brahmans, the Vedic priests.

The Vedic religion eventually evolved into Hinduism. Hindus worship a total of 330 million gods (demons), with each position in yoga giving reverence to one of those gods (demons). Yoga, karate and other occultist practices are now widely accepted by many churches, with believers attempting to remove the pagan aspects of each practice in an attempt to "not put away their pagan gods." This is similar to taking an altar out of a pagan temple, wiping the blood off that altar, taking it into a church, and then, offering contaminated sacrifices to God from that altar. By bringing occultism into the church, Jezebel is attempting to bewitch and discredit Christianity as a whole. You see, we cannot cry out about pagan practices without having an unbeliever point out the fact that we are practicing paganism! Many pseudo-intellectuals are rising up and challenging Christians head-on and some of them are pointing out facts! The world wants to discredit the church and we are helping them do it by accepting their rituals while attempting to reject their gods.

Ahab'ing the Church
What does it mean to "ahab" the church? Remember,

Ahab was king of Israel and God referred to the Israelites as His people. When Ahab made Jezebel queen, he gave her power and authority over God's people. Basically, he gave darkness authority over light and this was illegal! And when darkness had authority over the light, it started casting out anything that represented the light. When Jezebel became queen, she turned the heart of Ahab and the Israelites to Baal and then, she started killing off God's prophets! This was reverse deliverance whereas the devil was now casting God out of His own people. This is what Jezebel is working towards today. She's managed to ahab our government; she's managed to ahab our schools, but the real power is in the church. Right now, Jezebel has eunuchs stationed in many churches and these souls have their cell-phones on record, looking to "expose" another man or woman of God. They look for darkness and if they cannot find any, they record "snippets" of sermons designed to make the pastors look like hateful, noninclusive bigots with a thirst for blood. After this, they seek to make their videos go viral so their own names can be known at the expense of the church. Basically, they have made a deal with the devil and many of them don't even know this. In exchange for an opportunity to bring down another man or woman of God, Satan promises them fame, power and sometimes, wealth. These eunuchs and low-level Jezebels are responsible for so many churches being closed, so many pastors committing suicide and so many victories for the kingdom of darkness against Christianity (but not Christ, of course). *Christianity is the established worship of Christ.* Because of this, many leaders are afraid to preach against controversial issues like abortion, homosexuality, and the right to discipline our children. This means that unfortunately, some leaders have successfully been ahab'ed, but there are some who Satan cannot get to bow to him because he does not have access to their outer courts and they cast him down every time he rises up and challenges their thoughts. They are unyielding, courageous believers who are willing to give their lives for the gospel. What makes them dangerous to Satan is ... they do not thirst for power or wealth; they simply love God and hate evil.

1 Kings 19:18 (ESV): *Yet I will leave seven thousand in Israel, all the knees that have not bowed to Baal, and every mouth that has not kissed him.*

James 1:14-15 (ESV): *But each person is tempted when he is lured and enticed by his own desire. Then desire when it has conceived gives birth to sin, and sin when it is fully grown brings forth death.*

What we are witnessing is a great rebellion against the Word of God or, better yet, a Jezebellion. The highest ranking principality over the United States, besides Mammon (the love of money), is the Jezebel principality.

How the Jezebellion Works

There are many believers out there who don't understand soul ties and for this reason, they are casual in their dealings with people. They don't realize how easy it is to establish a soul tie with a person and that's why there are so many hurting people on the face of this earth today. Jezebel works through soul ties. Of course, the Jezebel spirit does not have to establish a soul tie to operate, but it operates best when it has a soul tie.

Our souls are comprised of our mind, will and emotions. A soul tie is when a person's mind (heart) is accessible to another person, oftentimes through familiarity. You won't have a soul tie with a person you don't know. Let's revisit the example of you being in church and being questioned by a woman you don't know. She wants to know the whereabouts of the pastor. She has engaged your conscious mind, but she cannot affect your life's decisions because there is no intimacy between you and her. However, if that same woman was to prophesy to you and you believed the words she spoke, you will open yourself to a soul tie with her. Now, you can understand why Jezebel loves and employs false prophets.

If the member started prophesying to you, you will open yourself up to receive or consider her words. If you don't receive her words as true, but instead, decide to

275

test the prophecy, the woman's words will sit on the outer courts of your subconscious. This is the waiting room of your heart or, better yet, your belief system. If you pray and you patiently wait for an answer from God, He will reveal whether the prophecy came from Him or not. If it did not, it's still in the holding cell of your mind so you can easily cast it down. However, if you are impatient or if what she has spoken to you is what you want to hear and you receive it as true, it will enter the outer courts of your heart and start making its way to the inner courts. It will then begin to affect your decision-making. If it turns out that the prophecy was not from God, you won't be able to cast it down anymore; instead, it'll have to be cast out. This means that you'll have to go through deliverance from the doctrine and the demons that came with the doctrine.

On my bi-weekly prayer calls, I normally perform deliverance at the end of the calls and one of the demons I call out is "demons that came in through false prophecies." Sure enough, the moment its name is called out, it manifests. My prayer calls usually consist of anywhere between 100 to 300 people, depending on the subject of the call, and the deliverance portion can be very noisy. When *demons who came in through false prophecies* are called out, it is not unusual to hear people coughing, wheezing and vomiting. That's because Satan accessed their hearts by telling them something they wanted to hear. For example, if a woman is anxious to get married, someone with a spirit of divination may approach her and tell her, for example, that some man at her church is her God-appointed husband. If she is anxious and does not test this prophecy, she may find herself becoming emotionally soul tied to the man, even though she does not know him. What this means is ... his choices will have the ability to affect her choices. His choices will be able to affect her mind, will, and emotions. So, if she sees the man for three months and he never approaches her, it's going to affect her in a negative way. This opens her up for further demonic infestation by opening her to the spirits of rejection, loneliness, and divination. She may start having dreams about the man and dreams about having his children. These beliefs will invade her conscious and work horizontally to control every aspect of her subconscious mind. They may even provide a platform for other demonic spirits to enter her subconscious mind and her body if she is not delivered. This is why Jezebel loves and adores ungodly soul ties. They allow her to control people and they allow her to cause people to self-destruct. They also allow her to establish demonic networks (kingdoms) in the people she binds. I've met many women who were convinced that some of the men they'd come in contact with were their God-appointed husbands, even though those men had expressed no interest in them. This demonic enslavement kept the women bound for years on end, suffering one disappointment after the next. In some cases, the women did get romantically involved with the guys and because they were convinced that the men were their husbands, they ended up compromising their souls even further through fornication. After that, the men walked away, leaving them confused, broken, uncovered, and open for more demonic invasion. I remember one woman telling me that her leader had prophesied to her that a certain man was her husband. The problem was ... the man was already married. Because she believed the woman, she entertained the man's adulterous ways, but I don't think they ever had sex because of the distance between them. Eventually, he did divorce his wife, but to her surprise, he immediately went and married another woman. When she approached her leader about this, she told her that he'd disobeyed God, so God would provide her with another husband. The girl in question eventually turned away from Christianity.

Demons cannot reside in a believer's spirit, therefore, they have to enter in through the soulish realm. This is why soul ties are so important to Jezebel. Ungodly soul ties allow Jezebel and other demonic entities to gain access to a person's mind, will, and emotions. If a demon can inspire how you think, it can control the weather of your emotions. If it can control your emotions, it can get behind the "will" of your life. For example, let's say that you've planned a great day for you and your husband. It's Saturday and the two of you are off work, plus, your sister volunteered to watch your children for the weekend. You've planned a romantic day with your husband and the both of you are excited about it. Let's say, for example's sake, that your ex-boyfriend and the father of your oldest child has the Jezebel spirit and he decides to call you. Your phone rings just as you and your husband are heading out your living room door. Your ex is livid because he saw your sister at the local park with his daughter and he starts accusing you of never having time for your own daughter. You know that this isn't true and you know how your ex is. He's still angry that you've moved on and he's been looking for some type of way to sabotage your marriage by constantly calling and complaining about everything you do. Plus, he knows how to provoke you. He tells you that he's going to go and see his lawyer on Monday morning and file for custody of your daughter. At that moment, you're overcome with anger, fear, and frustration. You're emotionally riled up and so is your husband. Instead of going on the romantic date you've planned, the two of you decide to spend the day at home, researching custody lawyers and talking about his intentions. Do you see how your ex's demons were able to get behind the "will" of your emotions and stop you from doing what you'd planned to do? This is why Satan loves and adores ungodly soul ties. Even though he can't possess or control believers, he can become their emotional weatherman if he has an ungodly person soul-tied to them or linked to them in any way.

Ungodly soul ties give Satan direct access to a person's belief system. For example, most of what your parents said to you did not have to rest in the outer courts of your heart when you were a child. You believed everything they said. However, when you got older, you started questioning a lot of what they said and this is when you entered the infamous "teenage rebellion." This is when you didn't receive their words as truth anymore; instead, their words were put to the test and oftentimes, rejected. You did this because you started cleaning out your inner courts and casting out what you believed were childish beliefs.

1 Corinthians 13:11 (ESV): *When I was a child, I spoke like a child, I thought like a child, I reasoned like a child. When I became a man, I gave up childish ways.*

Whenever you felt that your parents were treating you like a child, you rejected their words because the old beliefs were now gone and they had no foundation to stand on and no magnet-belief to attach themselves to.

A magnet-belief is a belief that attracts similar beliefs. This is similar to what Jezebel does to immature believers. She first causes them to question the Word of God and the origin of the Bible. This is her attempt to cast out every good and true belief; this way, she can start importing ungodly beliefs into the believer. When this process starts initially, believers begin to question the authenticity of their Bibles and then, they begin to question their leaders. Remember, Satan deceived Eve by simply asking her a question. This question was designed to get her to open up the inner courts of her thinking so that he could plant seeds. Once she considered or, better yet, opened herself up to his suggestions, he then told her what to believe. This is the virus of deception and it's designed to take down everyone that the deceived person has access to.

Genesis 3:1-7 (ESV): *Now the serpent was more crafty than any other beast of the field that the Lord God had made. He said to the woman, "Did God actually say, 'You shall not eat of any tree in the garden'?" And the woman said to the serpent, "We may eat of the fruit of the trees in the garden, but God said, 'You shall not eat of the fruit of the tree that is in the midst of the garden, neither shall you touch it, lest you die.'" But the serpent said to the woman, "You will not surely die. For God knows that when you eat of it your eyes will be opened, and you will be like God, knowing good and evil." So when the woman saw* *that the tree was good for food, and that it was a delight to the eyes, and that the tree was to be desired to make one wise, she took of its fruit and ate, and she also gave some to her husband who was with her, and he ate. Then the eyes of both were opened, and they knew that they were naked. And they sewed fig leaves together and made themselves loincloths.*

Here's the way that the Jezebellion works. Everyone is connected to someone and everyone has established beliefs. Every person in our lives who is familiar to and familiar with us has some level of access to the inner courts of our thinking. This includes our co-workers, even though we may not necessarily believe everything they say. Nevertheless, they can and do affect our emotions, which is one of the layers of our soul. Every belief that we have is contagious and we share those beliefs with any and everyone who opens themselves up to hear from us. If our beliefs are ungodly and the people we are speaking with do not immediately receive what we've said, but have given us personal (familiar) access to them, we can successfully plant seeds in them. And just as mustard-seed-sized faith can cause a mountain to move, a mustard seed's worth of doubt has the potential to move a mountain of blessings away from you. This is why it is very important to the Jezebel spirit to get you to open up your life to people who employ seducing spirits. Their assignments aren't necessarily to gain full access to the inner courts of your thinking; sometimes, they simply need enough access to you to plant seeds in your life. For example, one message I taught was called "Witchcraft by Proxy." In "Witchcraft by Proxy," I explained how the Jezebel spirit successfully gets true believers to pray against true believers. A good example is ... you happen to be friends with a guy named Chuck. One day, the Lord tells you to separate yourself from Chuck because Chuck has entered full-blown rebellion, meaning, darkness has seared a lot of Chuck's mind. Because of this, Chuck doesn't have much wisdom to share with you. Instead, any communications with him from there on out would be his fervent attempts to change your mind.

Proverbs 13:20 (ESV): *Whoever walks with the wise becomes wise, but the companion of fools will suffer harm.*

You finally obey God and take your distance from Chuck who, by the way, has a passive demeanor and a puppy-dog face to match. People who are close to Chuck know how deceptive and manipulative he is, but people who don't know him think he's harmless. You and Chuck are new members at the same church and Chuck's not too happy to see you every Sunday sitting in the ministers' section. Nevertheless, Chuck had a plan even before you disassociated yourself from him. He'd already started contacting every minister who was personal to you and tried to gain personal, intimate access to them. He has been successful a few times because of his puppy-dog eyes and his ability to *sound* teachable.

Chuck begins to contact one of the ministers who sits closest to you at church. So that his motives won't be clearly seen, Chuck initially says to him, "I have a question. I won't say any names because I am a man of integrity, but a former good friend of mine just cut me off because I wouldn't do what he told me to do. I don't know what to do. I'm hurt because I really thought he was my friend and even though he could be a bit controlling, I was sure that he was a man of God, especially since he's a minister here. What should I do? My heart is hurting and I don't want to disappoint God." Everyone at your church knows that you're Chuck's only friend. What Chuck has done is sown a seed and passively pointed you out. This is Chuck's attempt to destroy your character and get you cast out of the church or, at minimum, your leader's good grace. He then starts lying to a few members and saying you've been praying against him, so basically, he starts selling the idea that you are sending out witchcraft prayers, which is not true. If they buy into this lie, Chuck may successfully get them to send out prayers against you. This is *witchcraft by proxy*, whereas, the enemy has managed to get people to pray while deceived. This can be dangerous and it is one of the many witchcraft tools you'll find in Jezebel's bag of tricks. What Chuck has done is employed seducing spirits to accomplish his agenda. What's even worse is if Chuck is convinced you are in error and that his lies about you are God-approved.

This is why God told us to test the spirits and not just the spirits that are in others, but every spirit that is operating in our lives. If Chuck had access to you, more than likely, there was something unclean in you—some darkness that allowed what was in Chuck to hide in your life. However, the more you submitted yourself to God, the more deliverance you received. The more deliverance you received, the more the light of God begin to shine in what were once dark areas of your life and heart. Eventually, this light exposed Chuck and it gave you the ability to cast him out of your life. Understand this: just like we have to be delivered from demonic spirits, we have to be delivered from people who have demonic spirits.

Our connections are important to God because just like an extension cord, they allow power to enter and exit our lives. This means it is important *who* we are connected to and *how* we are connected to them. For example, people often argue that Jesus sat and ate with unbelievers and while this is true, we must understand the *way* He was connected. Connections are important, but *the way we connect* is more important than who we connect with. Jesus wasn't going into ungodly places with them or using their language. He did not compromise who He is to reach them. Instead, they followed after Him to access the God in Him. He was the one making the deposit. It was power leaving His body and wisdom leaving His mind and being transferred to them. They weren't able to secularize Him or get Him to agree with their points of view. This means that He acted as the power source (minister) while they plugged in to receive power. Many believers entertain ungodly associations where their friends and families aren't receiving wisdom, knowledge or understanding from them. As a matter of fact, they are made to feel scared or ashamed to talk about Christ while in their friends or family's presence, so they make subtle remarks about Him to justify staying connected to them. They may even convince their "connections" to come to church with them a few times. What they have is an establishment where they are on the receiving end of the connection and they are receiving what's on the inside of the folks they refuse to disconnect from. This is how the Jezebel spirit spreads itself out.

In the world of politics and media, Jezebel has established spiritual wickedness in high places by choosing the people she wants to be influential. Jezebel's goal is to grow her own influence, so she will choose the candidate in politics who's most compromised, has the most secrets or is the most fearful. In the media world, she chooses the most desperate candidates whose consciences are already seared or have the potential to be seared because of their lack of godly submission. She also chooses the most wicked candidates—people who are already filled with high-ranking demonic spirits. She then uses these people to act similar to principalities. They control the beliefs, laws, fads, and fashions of this world. Some of today's musical artists are responsible for many of the children that have been born. How so? It was their music that opened up the men and women to fornication and it was their music that attracted them to certain people. For example, the more celebrated a celebrity is, the more that celebrity's facial features will be idolized and revered as "handsome" or "beautiful." If the celebrity happens to be a man, a lot of men who look like him will suddenly begin to receive attention. Before long, you'll notice an influx of women having babies by men who look like the celebrity they've idolized. Some of them will even name their child or children after their idols. This is just to demonstrate how powerful the media is, especially the music industry.

Jezebel doesn't have to have personal access to a person; she simply needs access to their ear-gates and eye-gates. Person-to-person connections are important to her, but she doesn't necessarily need them. She simply needs a way to access the inner courts of a person's thinking and by raising up celebrities and influential government officials, she can control the masses and spread out her witchcraft.

The Jezebel spirit's influence has grown in the United States so much so that we are now self-destructing from within. We don't need a war to take us out because we are now attacking ourselves and one another. The United States has now become the divided states of America. Hatred and ignorance have divided us. Because of our greed and lust for power, we have allowed people to bring their gods into the country and then rebel against our God. We have allowed terrorists into our country and we have personally trained them to wage effective wars against us. We are planning wars while our enemies are engaging in warfare. We have joined hands with a false love that we are so affectionately referring to as "inclusion" and this false love has even started searing the minds of many believers.

Matthew 24:24 (ESV): *For false christs and false prophets will arise and perform great signs and wonders, so as to lead astray, if possible, even the elect.*

We have entered the great Jezebellion and we are witnessing our ahab'ed nation attempt to ahab the church. Nevertheless, in the midst of us are Elijahs hiding in caves, Jehus who haven't been sent out yet and men and women of God who will not bow to Baal. Of course, things will get worse, but we can rest assured that YAH-WEH will once again prove Himself to be the only true and living God. He will, once again, have Jezebel pushed off her high place and many of the people whose hearts are turned away from Him will eventually say, "The Lord, he is God; the Lord, he is God."

CHAPTER 9

Self Deliverance

I was driving when I suddenly heard the Lord speak. He said, "Now, go back and take responsibility for every wrong thing that has ever happened to you since you were an adult." I smiled and my heart began to dance with excitement. He was talking about this book. I'd shared *some* of my encounters with Jezebel and how God delivered me from people who had the Jezebel spirit. Now, there I was being told to go back and assume the responsibility for *everything* Jezebel has *ever done* to the *adult* me. I smiled for several reasons. The first reason was ... the first time I've ever heard Him say this was when I was going through my second divorce. Both of my marriages failed because of my exes' choices. They'd both had adulterous affairs and I'd gone through a lot with them. Nevertheless, during the first year of the second marriage, I'd finally surrendered my heart, mind, and soul to God. I stopped being double-minded, I repented for my sins, and I let God lead me through that marriage. So when He told me to take responsibility for the failure of both marriages, He gave me a level of un derstanding, compassion, and love that surpassed my human reasoning. Sure, the guys were responsible for the *ending* of those marriages, but I was responsible for the *beginning* of them. He explained it this way: He said that if I'd obeyed Him and not married the men I'd married, I would never have endured a divorce. The marriages were my fault because I did not get married against my will, and the divorces were my fault because I went into both marriages fully knowing that the men were not saved. I tried to lead them to Christ and this was out of order. This was a jezebellic move; it was spiritual pedophilia because God called the husband to be the head of his own home. Even though I'd married the first time when I was but a babe in Christ, I still knew better. The evidence to this is the fact that I did not consult with my pastor before getting married, nor did I introduce him to the man I was marrying. I *am not saying* that you need your pastor's permission to get married. I *am saying* that if God has appointed someone to serve as your pastor, you should trust them to watch over your soul; that way, you don't end up soul-tied to the wrong people. If you don't trust them, why are you seated under them? The truth is ... we forsake our pastors when we forsake the counsel of the Most High God. This happens when we are led astray by our own lusts and desires. This happens when we are bound by the spirit of rebellion. At that time in my life, I was so determined to marry my ex that I wouldn't even listen to God. I just wanted what I wanted when I wanted it. I thought I could go back and make things right with God once I'd gotten settled into my marriage.

When the Lord had me to take responsibility for the failure of those marriages, He led out of a prison cell called "blame." Sure, I could point out their wrongdoings and shortcomings. I could even tell you countless stories of me being the victim, but doing so would only mean that I haven't accepted *my* role in what happened to me. For example, I survived a very violent rape attempt when I was 19 years old. I'd gone to a man's house after he'd called me at work to let me know that he was in town. At first, I told him that I wasn't coming because I was engaged to get married, but when he told me that he'd brought me some jewelry from overseas, I started reasoning within myself that I'd go to his house, talk with him for a few minutes, get the jewelry, and leave. I knew the guy liked me. I knew that he was going to try to have sex with me, but I thought that he'd respect my "no," give me the jewelry, and I'd go home. It didn't end that way. I left his house shaken up, with scarring around my neck, and no jewelry. Was he guilty of trying to rape me? *Yes.* Was I an innocent victim? *No.* I'd made one unwise choice after the other. Even though I shared the blame with him (because he was guilty of his role in the attempted rape), I assumed the bulk of the responsibility, and that's what kept me from making that same mistake again.

Taking responsibility for everything that happened to the adult me didn't mean that I was declaring everyone else innocent of their crimes. What it meant was I'd accepted my role in those crimes and I'd come to understand that I was not the judge, jury, or prosecutor in any of those cases. I had to take responsibility for the things that happened to me in my friendships, associations and my romantic relationships. For example, Nancy didn't hold a gun to my head and force me to talk or deal with her. Sure, she was forceful, but I still had the freedom of will. Nevertheless, I was bound by a bunch of self-imposed rules and it was those rules that led me into captivity. I'd created those rules in my own attempt to not do to others what had been done to me, and then, I proceeded to become legalistic in regards to my own rules. I didn't leave any room for the voice of the Holy Spirit, nor did I leave any room for good ole common sense. What I didn't understand was ... I didn't need new rules. I needed to follow the Word of God; that would have been enough to keep me.

One of the keys to deliverance is accountability. You may have been stalked by the Jezebel spirit or you may be bound by the Jezebel spirit, but ask yourself this: what could I have done to prevent myself from going through what I've gone through? If you're honest with yourself and others, you'll notice how different the story sounds when you accept responsibility for your mistakes. If Jezebel has been stalking you, it's likely because you need to be delivered from the Ahab spirit. Ahab is not an innocent victim; he is the reason that Jezebel became queen over Israel. The same is true when dealing with the Jezebel-Ahab duo. Anytime we forsake deliverance, disobey the Word of God, and enter rebellion, we will find ourselves face-to-face with Jezebel because we will have wandered off into her region. Consider this example: an obviously wealthy woman instructs her limo driver to take her into a seedy area of town. She spots a gang of men drinking and gambling near a liquor store. She then tells her driver to stop the car and she proceeds to leave the safety of her vehicle and approach the men. "Can you tell me how to get to 44th Street?" she asks. All of a sudden, one of the men pull out a gun and demand that she hand over her purse. Whose fault is this? Every man who participated in robbing that woman is guilty of robbery, but she is guilty of not using the common sense that the good Lord gave her. If she does not accept her role in the robbery, she'll likely wander off into another seedy area and proceed to ask for directions again, but this time, she may not live to report the crime.

When God had me to assume responsibility for my failed marriages, my life changed for the better. I'd already forgiven the guys, but taking accountability for my own wrongs, caused the shackles of blame to fall off me and it helped me to enter a new level of love and compassion. There, I found new wisdom waiting for me. There, I found a new set of eyes. This has forever changed my perspective and my life. So, assuming the responsibility for what I *allowed* Jezebel to take me through only means that I've chosen to not only learn from my mistakes but to grow from them. Many people are what is best described as spiritual midgets because they've stopped growing long ago. Instead, they spend their lives pointing the finger of blame at everyone who's ever hurt them, walked away from them, or in some cases, told them a truth that they did not want to hear. I've met countless people like this and one thing they all have in common is ... they are stuck and they can never seem to move forward. Year after year, they stand around and collect stories where they are always the victim and never the offender nor the victor. This is how bitterness sets in. We have to learn from our mistakes, otherwise, we will become living lessons for others to learn from. The point is ... deliverance and promotion start with accountability. Once we accept our roles in the things that we've gone through, we can move on to the next level of wisdom, knowledge, and understanding.

Next, to break Jezebel's curse in your life, you need to look for the root of Jezebel's presence in your life. What led you into captivity? Please understand that everything has a root attached to it. For example, the root of promiscuity for many women is the fact that they were molested. If I were to teach those women that God wanted them to walk in holiness and they were to stop fornicating, there would be no true victory in their lives. Basically, telling them to stop fornicating without dealing with the root of their fornication is similar to telling a demon that you won't cast it out if it'll stop manifesting. Of course, the demon will agree to your terms, and it may go a long time without acting up, but it's a demon. This means that it won't be long before it starts acting like a demon again. The same is true for a promiscuous woman who suddenly embraces abstinence without dealing with the root of her promiscuity. What would happen to her is ... the enemy would likely send a man into her life who agrees to be abstinent with her. She'd be deceived by his willingness to refrain from premarital sex (with her), and she could easily find herself married to the guy. After the vows are said, that man's demons will suddenly start manifesting. The blushing bride may find herself being beaten, ridiculed, and maybe even forced into prostitution by her new husband.

Where's the Entrance Door?

How did Jezebel get into your life? Is that spirit in your bloodline? Are the women in your family controlling, seductive and manipulative? Are the men in your family controlling, abusive, prideful and unstable? These questions are important because they help us to go back in time and address the entrance doors that Jezebel, Ahab and any other spirits under the Baal principality used to enter into our lives. Were you raped or molested? Did you work tirelessly to gain your parents' approval, only to find yourself being rejected by them time and time again?

One of the women that God blessed me to minister to had been dealing with a lot of warfare in her life. She was a meek and sweet young lady, but she kept finding herself in the grips of Jezebel. Not long after we started the counseling, she finally opened up and started confiding in me about a relative who'd repeatedly molested her when she was a child. He'd not only molested her, but he was still trying to control her. One day, she decided to confront him about what he'd done and what he was still doing. Of course, he did not want to take responsibility for his own wrongs, but this confrontation gave her the confidence that she needed to start confronting others in her family and her life who saw her as nothing but their own personal tool. I have no doubt that someday, God will use that same young woman to minister to other women. She didn't just acknowledge the demons; she started confronting them.

Knowing the entrance the demonic spirits used to enter your life is vital to staying free. Sure, you can kick the devil out of your life, but if there's an entrance door that allows him back in, he'll come back with seven spirits more wicked than the ones you evicted. You need to address the roots. For example, I was able to look over my childhood and see Ahab operating in my family. I've also witnessed the Jezebel spirit operating in my family, but not as much as the Ahab spirit. I was ashamed of this for many years, but God delivered me from the shame and taught me to walk in my God-given authority. He taught me how to get rid of the rules I'd created and He helped me to understand the reason I'd created those rules in the first place. I was trying to be safe in everything, which meant that I was not tapping into faith. Sure, rules are important in life, ministry, and business, but rules are designed to keep out lawlessness, not bind the lawmaker. Anytime you are bound by your own rules, you are bound (period).

Generational Curses

If the root of Jezebel's strongman in your life is generational, you need to renounce the bloodline curse. If your mother was abusive towards you, for example, more than likely she was bound by the infamous Jezebel spirit. This doesn't mean you have to confront her (unless God says otherwise); what it means is you need to confront the Jezebel spirit operating in your life. Confront it by first accepting everything that's happened in your adult life, and then, start freeing everyone the Jezebel spirit has used you to bind.

To break the generational curses in your life, you need to:
1. Renounce the bloodline curses and cancel them out of your life. Renunciation is done audibly, not inwardly.
2. Stay away from family members who don't want to be free. It's easy to return to the Egypt that God has delivered you from if you have to keep going there to visit the folks that you call family. What I've learned is that the best way for a person to save their family is by that person first getting free, walking out that freedom consistently, and staying tuned in to the voice of God. Slowly, but surely, God will use that person to lead every bound person in their family to freedom who *wants* to be free. I had a dream some years ago when I was married to Roger. Before the dream, Roger and I had flown into the

States, and we were staying at Mara's house. We were supposed to stay there for a few months because Roger had gotten a new job, but his position wouldn't be available to him for several months. I wanted to stay at my mother's house, but Roger insisted on us staying with Mara. From the minute we walked into Mara's house, I knew that our marriage wasn't going to survive if we stayed there. Mara wouldn't speak to me, nor would she even acknowledge my presence unless she wanted to scold me about something. She'd began to escalate her attack against me, so she worked tirelessly to keep Roger away from me. If I was in a room with Roger, she'd call him out of it. If I was in the kitchen, she'd tell me what not to touch. If I turned on the fan (it was over 90°F outside and Mara would not turn on her air conditioner), she'd tell me that she was going to give her electric bill to me. She'd then proceed to turn off the fan and then, fan herself with one of her handmade fans. I was in a living hell and I knew I couldn't take much more of it. Roger and I had planned to visit my mother for a couple of weeks and before we went, Mara stopped Roger and told him that I could go, but he wasn't allowed to leave. This was one of the few times when Roger did not listen to Mara. We flew out to Mississippi and everything was peaceful at my mother's house. I begged Roger for us to stay in Mississippi until his job started, but he kept talking about culture and how disrespectful it would be if we didn't return to Mara's house. We argued about it daily and I prayed fervently because I knew I could not endure staying with Mara for long.

One night, I dreamed that Roger and I were waking up on a couch. We had the masks on our faces that hospitals put on people to administer oxygen and gas to them. In the dream, Roger and I were just waking up. I woke up (in the dream) knowing that Roger and I were in captivity, even though we were seated on a couch. I understood that the masks had sleeping gas in them.

As we opened our eyes, I saw the woman from the movie *Misery* sitting in front of us. She was sitting on a wooden chair facing us and immediately, I had an understanding. I understood that this was her third time capturing us and we'd escaped the first two times. And even though she had the face of the woman from the movie *Misery*, I understood the woman to be Mara and that was how I addressed her in the dream. Lastly, I understood that the woman had a lot of large black cats (I think they were black panthers) and she'd tried to feed us to them before, but we'd gotten away. I knew that she was about to try and feed us to them again. Amazingly enough, I didn't see the black cats in the dream, but somehow, I knew that she had a few of them.

I immediately started trying to be friendly with the woman, hoping that she'd release us. She chatted with us briefly, and at first, it appeared that my kind words were working on her, but I was wrong. Without warning, she smiled at us and said that she had to go and get the cats ready. She leaned in to put the masks back over our faces and somehow, I communicated with Roger to tilt his head so he wouldn't breathe in the gas. I told him to pretend to be asleep and I would do the same.

Moments later, we were seated in a kitchen with a lot of women. I understood that Mara was in the back getting the cats ready and those women all worked for her. They were chatting amongst themselves, laughing and obviously not paying too much attention to Roger and I. I noticed an open door behind me, so again, I silently communicated to Roger. I told him that I was going to count to three and run out of that door. I told him to run with me. I counted to three and then, took off running out of the door. I was running down a long street and I looked behind me to see if Roger was following me, but he wasn't. I panicked, but I didn't stop running.

I ran into a small store and started screaming at the cashier. I told him about the kidnapping and I told him that my husband was still at the kidnapper's house. I asked for a phone to call the police and he gave it to me.

While on the phone with the police department, Roger suddenly ran through the door of the store. I hugged him and told him the police were on the way. That's when I suddenly woke up from that nightmare.

Our flight was scheduled to leave the following day. We were supposed to be returning to Mara's house from Mississippi. I understood what God was telling me in the dream. Truly, that visit had been our third visit to Mara's house and each time, she'd tried to destroy our marriage. After I hadn't agreed to the "masseuse offer" she'd made, she'd changed for the worst. I told Roger to take the flight back on his own and try to work things out with Mara. I told him that I'd fly back in two to three weeks and that would give him enough time to find out why Mara hated me so much. He let out a sigh of relief and agreed. I knew that God was telling me that I would escape Mara's grip first, but Roger would escape later.

For three weeks, Roger and I lived in two different states. We talked daily and he tried to resolve whatever problem Mara had with me. Nevertheless, Mara was unrelenting. I knew that she wasn't going to accept me as I was; she wanted to control me like she controlled everyone around her, but I wouldn't let her. I couldn't let her.

The day before I was supposed to fly back to the state

Mara was in, I had a dream, but it was a weird dream because I had it just as I was waking up, plus, I didn't see anything. Instead, I was having a conversation with God and He told me that Mara was going to tell Roger that she didn't want me to come back to her house. He told me to tell Roger to come back to Mississippi. That's when I woke up.

I don't remember if Roger called me or I called Roger, but we talked almost immediately after I woke up and I said to him that Mara was going to tell him that she wanted me to stay in Mississippi for the next few months and he was to stay with her. I reminded him that we (he and I) were married and I said, "If she says that she doesn't want me to come to her house, I want you to come back to Mississippi. It's not right for a husband and wife to separate." Roger became angry. "She won't say that!" he shouted. Nevertheless, there was a calm around me and in me that I could not explain. I didn't argue with him. I just reiterated what I said and I told him that I'd buy his ticket to come back since he hadn't started working yet. We got off the phone, and I went about my normal day.

Later that day, I got a call from Roger. "Please buy my ticket," he said. "I'll call you to explain later." I was excited. He'd told me to buy him a bus ticket instead of a plane ticket to save money and he told me what date he wanted me to buy the ticket for. I rushed to the computer and purchased the ticket. I couldn't help but to go and glorify God because He had surely worked it out, but first, I had to obey Him.

Roger called later that day and told me that Mara had come home from work and she'd brought a woman with her. She then proceeded to tell him that she didn't want me back at her house because I would not "listen" to her and she told him that she wanted him to stay with her until his job started. She said, "Tiffany can stay in Mississippi with her mother and you will stay here with me." Roger disagreed and the two of them argued. That's when the woman she'd brought home spoke up and started telling him the importance of blood (family). She told him to listen to Mara, but he didn't. About a week later, Roger was back in town and we ended up staying with my mother until he started his job.

Sadly enough, Roger physically got away from Mara, but he didn't get away from her spiritually. She continued to control him for the duration of our marriage and she'd even introduced him to another woman. Eventually, our marriage gave way and Roger finally left.

The point is ... if you don't get away from people who

love their demons, they will cost you almost everything you have. Roger was a decent guy, but he needed some major deliverance. He lost a lot trying to appease Mara when, in truth, there is no way to appease a demonic spirit. Thankfully, because I forgave him, God used me to lead Roger through the sinner's prayer while we were going through a divorce.

Forgiveness

One of the keys to freedom is releasing others. The same is true for the Ahab spirit. If you're operating under the Ahab spirit, you may have misjudged the people who God sent to be the Elijah and the Micaiah prophets in your life. You need to forgive them, cancel out every evil and negative word you've spoken against them, and then, release them. If you've spread rumors about them, you need to clear up those rumors. If you've hurt or offended them, you need to apologize directly to them. I understand that this may be uncomfortable, but it is necessary. At the same time, once you get past the discomfort of it all and obey God, you will experience a peace that you haven't experienced in a long time. (Note: if they choose not to forgive you, you are free. God didn't say to go into bondage with anyone. He simply told us to repent to one another.)

Matthew 5:22-26 (ESV): *But I say to you that everyone who is angry with his brother will be liable to judgment;*

whoever insults his brother will be liable to the council; and whoever says, 'You fool!' will be liable to the hell of fire. So if you are offering your gift at the altar and there remember that your brother has something against you, leave your gift there before the altar and go. First be reconciled to your brother, and then come and offer your gift. Come to terms quickly with your accuser while you are going with him to court, lest your accuser hand you over to the judge, and the judge to the guard, and you be put in prison. Truly, I say to you, you will never get out until you have paid the last penny.

Next, if you owe someone something, you need to repay them. Debt gives the enemy permission to bind you if the people you owe won't release you. This is why God told us to forgive others for their debts. Sure, we can do this in our own personal lives, but some people don't know how to forgive others. This isn't an indictment against them; the truth is ... they simply just don't know because they've never seen a demonstration of forgiveness. So, if you've borrowed money from someone, stolen something from someone or promised something to someone, you need to work towards giving it back to them.

Proverbs 6:1-5 (ESV): *My son, if you have put up security for your neighbor, have given your pledge for a stranger, if you are snared in the words of your mouth,* *caught in the words of your mouth, then do this, my son, and save yourself, for you have come into the hand of your neighbor: go, hasten, and plead urgently with your neighbor. Give your eyes no sleep and your eyelids no slumber; save yourself like a gazelle from the hand of the hunter, like a bird from the hand of the fowler.*

Romans 13:8 (ESV): *Owe no one anything, except to love each other, for the one who loves another has fulfilled the law.*

Luke 11:2-4 (ESV): *And he said to them, "When you pray, say: "Father, hallowed be your name. Your kingdom come. Give us each day our daily bread, and forgive us our sins, for we ourselves forgive everyone who is indebted to us. And lead us not into temptation."*

If you haven't forgiven someone who's hurt you, you need to forgive them if you want to be forgiven by God. You cannot hold someone in bondage and expect God to set you free.

Matthew 6:12 (ESV): *...and forgive us our debts, as we also have forgiven our debtors.*

Matthew 18:21-35 (ESV): *Then Peter came up and said to him, "Lord, how often will my brother sin against me, and I forgive him? As many as seven times?" Jesus said to him, "I do not say to you seven times, but seventy-seven times. Therefore the kingdom of heaven may be compared to a king who wished to settle accounts with his* *servants. When he began to settle, one was brought to him who owed him ten thousand talents. And since he could not pay, his master ordered him to be sold, with his wife and children and all that he had, and payment to be made. So the servant fell on his knees, imploring him, 'Have patience with me, and I will pay you everything.' And out of pity for him, the master of that servant released him and forgave him the debt. But when that same servant went out, he found one of his fellow servants who owed him a hundred denarii, and seizing him, he began to choke him, saying, 'Pay what you owe.' So his fellow servant fell down and pleaded with him, 'Have patience with me, and I will pay you.' He refused and went and put him in prison until he should pay the debt. When his fellow servants saw what had taken place, they were greatly distressed, and they went and reported to their master all that had taken place. Then his master summoned him and said to him, 'You wicked servant! I forgave you all that debt because you pleaded with me. And should not you have had mercy on your fellow servant, as I had mercy on you?' And in anger his master delivered him to the jailers, until he should pay all his debt. So also my heavenly Father will do to every one of you, if you do not forgive your brother from your heart."*

Forgiveness is necessary for deliverance. Since I've entered deliverance ministry, I've found that the Jezebel spirit gains its strength from unforgiveness. I've had deliverance calls where people individually asked to be taken through deliverance. I remember one conference call in particular where I'd tried to take a woman through deliverance, but nothing happened. I was calling out the spirits, but they would not manifest. The line was silent and honestly, I was starting to feel silly constantly screaming, "Come out of her," and then, being faced with the reality that nothing was coming out. I was very new to deliverance then, so after 20 to 30 minutes of me screaming into the air, I finally told her to fast and ask the Lord why those spirits would not come out of her. She agreed. I then opened up the line and was able to take another woman through deliverance without resistance. I prayed about it and the Lord let me know that, of course, I was in error because I'd let her off the line without digging deeper and He ministered to me about her being in unforgiveness. During the next conference call, the same thing happened. One woman went through deliverance immediately, while another woman didn't have as much as a simple manifestation. Finally, I remembered what the Lord said to me and I started speaking with her about forgiveness. I told her that the demons would not come out of her unless she released the folks she was still holding captive. I told her to verbally declare that she'd forgiven each person (calling out their names) and then, to say that she was releasing each one of them. She did and not long after that, her deliverance took place without incident. If you don't forgive others, God won't forgive you, which means that you will disqualify yourself from receiving deliverance. One thing I've learned is ... a deliverance minister can call out demonic spirits when a person is in unforgiveness and the strongman may send out one of the demonic spirits to distract the deliverance minister. Howbeit, not only will the strongman open the door to let that demon back in, but it sent that spirit out to go and bring back seven spirits more wicked than itself. It is simply ensuring that the person does not seek deliverance again.

Forgive the folks who hurt you; release them and move forward. When the enemy tries to remind you of what they did to you, counter his attack by praying for them (not against them). Pray for their salvation (if they aren't saved) and pray for their deliverance. What you're doing is striking back against the kingdom of darkness by trying to free someone that the enemy once used to bind you.

Call Out the Strongman
Understand that in every demonic network, there is a strongman or ruling spirit. It is the "boss" of the network. It is possible to go through *some* deliverance from

demonic spirits without addressing or casting out the strongman, and when this happens, the strongman will let those spirits back in. Some people would argue that the Bible says in Mark 3:27 (ESV), "But no one can enter a strong man's house and plunder his goods, unless he first binds the strong man. Then indeed he may plunder his house." Some believe this to mean that a person cannot go through deliverance unless the strongman is first bound. Understand this: demons are intelligent (but foolish) creatures. If they can find legal grounds to stay in a person, they will not come out. Instead, they will work together to stop the deliverance or the deliverance attempt. If the deliverance minister has faith and is successfully disrupting them, they also know that God may start to instruct the minister and they don't want this. For this reason, it is easier to distract the minister by causing one or a few demons to come out or to make the person appear to be going through deliverance than it is to remain quiet while the deliverance minister keeps praying and calling them out. I've had times where I was calling spirits out of folks and sure enough, they were manifesting. Suddenly, the person would vomit and there would be quietness on the line. It sounded like the person was free and I wanted to believe that they were free, but I did not have a peace about it. No peace usually means the demons are still there. So, I would start praying and seeking the Lord for more instructions and when I would follow His instructions, the demons would start back manifesting.

How do you identify the strongman? Ask the Lord to tell you who it is. You can seek answers through fasting and prayer. Additionally, in most cases, God will tell the deliverance minister who the strongman is, but sometimes, the minister won't get to the strongman until he or she has bound up some of the spirits that come forth to defend the strongman. These guarding spirits usually include, but are not limited to: haughty spirit (pride), Leviathan, self pity, rage, witchcraft spirits, etc.

Lastly, understand that the word "plunder" references taking the good away from an enemy *after* you've overcome him. Demons aren't goods, therefore, the scripture references taking away that in which the enemy has stolen from you. Every good thing comes from God (James 1:17). What did the enemy steal? Remember, every good and bad mindset has a root and everything that has a root produces fruit. If you've been rejected, molested, raped, and attacked most of your life, the root of your bondage may be what you've gone through. It could have started off with parental rejection and that rejection may have led you to befriend someone you felt could serve as a parental figure in your life. That person ended up raping you and that rape led you to becoming hateful and promiscuous. So, in this case, rejection would be the root. Everything else is just fruit. Demons will come in and begin to eat from the fruit that's growing in your life. They will also start choking out the godly fruit to ensure that the gardens they are sourcing from are not overridden by wheat.

Mark 4:15-20 (ESV): *And these are the ones along the path, where the word is sown: when they hear, Satan immediately comes and takes away the word that is sown in them. And these are the ones sown on rocky ground: the ones who, when they hear the word, immediately receive it with joy. And they have no root in themselves, but endure for a while; then, when tribulation or persecution arises on account of the word, immediately they fall away. And others are the ones sown among thorns. They are those who hear the word, but the cares of the world and the deceitfulness of riches and the desires for other things enter in and choke the word, and it proves unfruitful. But those that were sown on the good soil are the ones who hear the word and accept it and bear fruit, thirtyfold and sixtyfold and a hundredfold."*

To plunder the enemy means to take away the good after you've overcome him. What exactly would you be taking? The fruit of the Holy Spirit, of course! These are the gifts that God has given and made available to the believer, but the enemy convinced you to water the demonic garden with worry, doubt, gossip, slander, fornication, etc., instead of watering and sourcing from the garden that God has made available to you.

Galatians 5:16-24 (ESV): *But I say, walk by the Spirit, and you will not gratify the desires of the flesh. For the desires of the flesh are against the Spirit, and the desires of the Spirit are against the flesh, for these are opposed to each other, to keep you from doing the things you want to do. But if you are led by the Spirit, you are not under the law. Now the works of the flesh are evident: sexual immorality, impurity, sensuality, idolatry, sorcery, enmity, strife, jealousy, fits of anger, rivalries, dissensions, divisions, envy, drunkenness, orgies, and things like these. I warn you, as I warned you before, that those who do such things will not inherit the kingdom of God. But the fruit of the Spirit is love, joy, peace, patience, kindness, goodness, faithfulness, gentleness, self-control; against such things there is no law. And those who belong to Christ Jesus have crucified the flesh with its passions and desires.*

If you feel uncomfortable trying to perform deliverance on yourself, seek out a godly deliverance minister. Pray first so that God will lead you to the right ministry and the minister will be able to identify the strongman operating in your life.

Get Counseling

Before and after deliverance, it is always a good idea to get counseling. The reason for this is when we are bound by demonic personalities, those personalities will sometimes graft themselves into our own personalities. For this reason, it is hard for us to know our personality from the demonic personalities that once enslaved us. For example, I often talked about how easy it was for me to walk away from people. I prided myself in having what I called the "gift of goodbye." I thought this was strength, but it wasn't. It was fear; it was rejection, and it was pride. Those three spirits had me in their grips and until I dealt with them, I could not receive my full deliverance.

Christian counseling helps you to separate your personality from the personality of a demonic spirit. It helps you to understand why you process conflict the way that you do and it teaches you to face every Goliath that challenges you; that way, you don't end up bragging about being a pride-filled Ahab like I was.

Ask for Deliverance by Name

Sometimes, pride keeps folks from seeking deliverance. I've found that this is even true for some leaders. Some leaders don't know who to turn to for deliverance and some are too ashamed to admit that they need it. For this reason, many God-established leaders behave in un-godly ways.

It doesn't matter if you are a leader or not .... always seek deliverance when you need it. Ask God to connect you with the leaders He wants to connect you with and anytime you find yourself needing deliverance, reach out to one of them and ask them if they'd be willing to minister deliverance to you. More than likely, they will agree to it and arrange a time and a place for the ministry to take place. Don't be ashamed. Needing deliverance doesn't mean that you've done something silly like watching porn, cheating on your spouse, or setting someone's car on fire. Most deliverance ministers understand that you likely got bound by some small infraction that you were unaware of. For example, maybe someone hurt you and you thought you'd forgiven that person but you hadn't. Maybe you had unchecked road rage. Then again, one of your close connections may have went into rebellion and you didn't rebuke that person, nor did you disconnect when God told you to disconnect. Don't hinder yourself worrying about what the leader or leaders will think about you. More than likely, if the minister is a humble, seasoned deliverance minister, he or she won't look for ways to accuse you. Instead, the minister will only be concerned about casting out whatever demon has gotten into you. It takes a whole lot of humility to admit that you need to be set free when you are in leadership. God made it this way so we would stay humble.

If you're not in leadership, speak with your pastor and try to arrange a meeting for you and whatever people he or she uses in the ministry of deliverance. Don't be ashamed. If your pastor does not believe that Christians can have demons and therefore, doesn't perform deliverance ministry, ask the Lord to show you where you can go to receive this ministry.

Maintain Your Deliverance
One of the biggest mistakes believers tend to make is they get the devil cast out one time and they don't come back to receive any more deliverance. I remember when I went through my first deliverance. I thought that sealed the deal. I thought I wouldn't need any more deliverance for the rest of my life. I was wrong.

One day, I was sitting on my couch feeling the weight of depression. I didn't know why I felt so heavy and so sad, and I didn't have anyone to turn to for help. I had recently left the church I was in and I'd withdrawn myself from people altogether. At first, I sat there feeling sorry for myself. I could come up with a lot of reasons as to why I could feel sad, but none of them were the reasons

I was feeling the way I felt. The heaviness seemed to come out of nowhere and when I questioned why I felt the way I did, I couldn't think of any thing that had triggered that depression. That's when it dawned on me. I was dealing with a demonic spirit and I needed to go through deliverance. I immediately pulled up an article I'd read about self deliverance and I started taking myself through the steps of deliverance. Before long, I was rushing to my bathroom to spit up everything the Lord had me to call out. This happened before I entered the ministry of deliverance and one thing I've learned is that God will often teach you to take yourself through deliverance before He will use you to take others through deliverance.

Steps to Self Deliverance
Anytime I feel any negative emotion that threatens to choke out the fruit of peace in my life, I take myself through deliverance. I've learned that anything that contends with the fruit of the Holy Spirit is more than likely a demonic entity trying to grow its own garden. Here are the steps that I normally follow.

- Approach the altar of God in praise and worship. Worship Him for who He is and praise Him for His love and mercy.
  Psalms 100:4 (ESV): Enter his gates with thanksgiving, and his courts with praise! Give thanks to

him; bless his name!

- Next, confess your sins to Him and repent of those sins. This includes the sins that you are unaware of.

Psalms 19:12 (ESV): Who can discern his errors? Declare me innocent from hidden faults.

- Spend time telling Him how you feel and what you're going through. Tell Him what you're struggling with. One day, I'd done this and the Lord told me to grab a notebook and a pen. Every time I talked about how I felt, He had me to write down the key words. I had to write down everything that followed, "I feel...." When I looked at my notebook, I realized I'd written down the names of several demonic spirits including: rejection, depression, loneliness, etc. I used that list to call those spirits out and sure enough, one by one, they began to manifest and come out. It wasn't long before I was standing over my toilet, spitting up. After that was over, I truly felt like a new woman and my peace and joy were both immediately restored.

Revelation 12:11 (ESV): And they have conquered him by the blood of the Lamb and by the word of their testimony, for they loved not their lives even unto death.

- Break all covenants, curses, witchcraft prayers

sent out against you and cancel every evil word that's been sent out against you. After that's over, bind the spirits that came in through those covenants, curses, witchcraft prayers and evil words.

- Break all ungodly soul ties and release every person you've bound through those soul ties. After that's over, bind the spirits that came in through those soul times.
- Start calling those spirits out by name. If you don't know their names, call out their functions. For example, you can say, "Demons that cause depression, I command you to come out of me in the name of Christ Jesus. I renounce you and I take authority over you. Manifest and come out of me now in Jesus name." Don't forget to call out Jezebel, Athaliah, Ahab and every spirit under the Baal principality. Also, be sure to break every principality in your life. *Note: some people like to lay hands on themselves when calling spirits out. This isn't necessary, but it does work as well. When you start calling them out, you may find yourself swaying or feeling like you're about to lose your footing. This is normal in deliverance.* You can also start calling out demons in your bloodline, demons that affect your emotions, spirits of mind control, demons that came in

through unforgiveness, etc. Additionally, you can call them out of every part of your body; for example, demons hiding in your kidneys, behind your eyes, in your liver, etc. Sometimes, when I'm performing deliverance ministry on someone else, I will start feeling pain in certain parts of my body. This lets me know where the demon is trying to hide in them. That's when I'll call it out; for example, "Demons hiding in her neck, come out now in the name of Jesus Christ!" It never fails ... the demon will start manifesting and it'll come out of that person. It is also good to use scriptures when calling out spirits.

- You'll feel a peace once you're either fully free or when God wants you to stop. Sometimes, you have to go through several deliverances to get fully free. Once you feel this peace, ask the Lord to give you a fresh infilling of the Holy Spirit.

Please understand that every deliverance minister's method may vary, but as long as faith and Jesus are involved, demons have to come out. Study deliverance often and learn as much about it as you can. Be willing to let go of any thing and any person the Holy Spirit tells you to release.

Remember, take accountability for your role in everything that happened to the adult you. Forgive everyone and make maintaining your deliverance a priority in your life. Also, remember to cancel out every evil word you've released into someone else's life through gossip, slander, backbiting, etc. Lastly, release everyone that you've bound. You do this by resisting the temptation to control, manipulate or belittle others. You do this by taking responsibility for yourself. You do this by trusting God to lead, keep, and provide for you.

The Jezebel spirit is one of many demonic spirits in the Baal network, so don't just cast out Jezebel; the rest of them need to go to. Don't look for pity from others and don't feel sorry for yourself (as these two spirits will lead you back into captivity). Instead, break the curse of Jezebel in your life and cast every demonic spirit operating in your life into the abyss. Do this as often as necessary. Never get so prideful that you stop seeking deliverance and never get so accustomed to being the victim that you forsake the opportunity to be victorious.

If you want to learn more about the Jezebel spirit, demonic governments and how to take others through deliverance, make sure that you get Volume II of Jezebellion. Volume II will teach you about demonic governments and how to advance into the ministry of deliverance.

Made in the USA
Coppell, TX
27 December 2024

43532068R00193